Darussalam International Publications Limited

Office : 0208 539 4885
Fax: 020 8181 6544
Web : www.darussalam.com
Email : info@darussalam.com

Prinded by Mega Printing in Turkey

TAWBAH:
TURNING TO ALLAH IN REPENTANCE

Explained by Ibn Qayyim al-Jawziyyah
Translated by Abdul Ali Hamid

TABLE OF CONTENTS

FOREWORD   6

CHAPTER ONE - FUNDAMENTALS OF REPENTANCE (TAWBAH)   10
SIGNIFICANCE OF REPENTANCE   10
REPENTANCE COMES WITH THE GUIDANCE OF ALLAH   11
THE CONDITIONS OF REPENTANCE   13
THE ESSENTIAL COMPONENTS OF REPENTANCE   16

CHAPTER TWO - UNDERSTANDING THE DECREE OF ALLAH   20
MAKING EXCUSES FOR SINS   20
REFERRING THE MATTERS TO THE DECREE OF ALLAH   25
REALISATION OF THE DECREE OF ALLAH   27
CONFRONTING THE DECREE BY THE DECREE   28

CHAPTER THREE - INNER DIMENSIONS OF REPENTANCE   29
SECRETS OF REPENTANCE   29
REPENTANCE FROM REPENTANCE   30
PERSONAL EVALUATION OF SIN   38
REFLECTION ON SERVITUDE AND LORDSHIP   39
SUMMARY OF RULES ABOUT REPENTANCE   46
REPENTANCE FROM A SIN WHILE INSISTING ON ANOTHER   47
ADDITIONAL RULES RELATED TO REPENTANCE   48

CHAPTER FOUR - DILEMMA OF SINNING VS REPENTANCE   53
EVIL DEEDS DO NOT SPOIL THE GOOD ONES   53
THE CASE OF A PERSON WHO WAS UNABLE TO COMMIT A SIN   54
A DILEMMA OF A MAN WHO CRAVES FOR A SIN ALTHOUGH HE
INTENDS TO REPENT   56
THE DUES OF THE HUMAN BEINGS MUST BE PAID   57
DOES REPENTANCE ABSOLVE THE SIN?   58
WHO IS BETTER: A MAN WHO NEVER COMMITTED A SIN
OR THE ONE WHO COMMITTED A SIN THEN REPENTED?   60
A MAN WHO COMMITTED THE SIN THEN REPENTED IS BETTER   62
THE SIGNIFICANCE OF FIRM INTENTION AND PREVENTION FROM FUTURE SINS   68
SEEKING FORGIVENESS   69
THE TRUE ESSENCE OF SINCERE REPENTANCE   71
DIFFERENCE BETWEEN REMOVING THE MISDEEDS AND FORGIVING THE SINS   72

ALLAH RESPONDS TO THE REPENTANCE OF A SERVANT   73
THE BEGINNING AND THE END OF REPENTANCE   74

CHAPTER FIVE - CATEGORISATION OF SINS   75
THE DIVISION OF SINS INTO MAJOR AND MINOR   75
CORRECT UNDERSTANDING OF THE MAGNITUDE OF SINS   79

CHAPTER SIX - CATEGORY OF OFFENCES THAT NEED REPENTANCE   87
DISBELIEF   87
SHIRK OR ASCRIBING PARTNERS TO ALLAH (POLYTHEISM)   90
HYPOCRISY   96
DEFIANCE   108
TRANSGRESSION AND SINS   113
IMMORALITY   115
TO SPEAK ABOUT ALLAH WITHOUT KNOWLEDGE   115

CHAPTER SEVEN - THE SPECIFIC RULING OF REPENTANCE FOR SPECIFIC CASES   118
REPENTANCE RULES GOVERNING MISSED OBLIGATORY PRAYER (SALAH)   118
OPINION IN FAVOUR OF PERFORMING MISSED OBLIGATORY PRAYER (SALAH)   118
OPINION AGAINST PERFORMING MISSED OBLIGATORY PRAYER (SALAH)   120
THE CASE OF A PERSON WHO FINDS IT DIFFICULT TO REDRESS THE HARM   127
IS THERE A SIN FOR WHICH THERE IS NO REPENTANCE?   131
THE CASE OF A MAN WHO KILLED SOMEONE AND WAS KILLED IN RETALIATION   136

CHAPTER EIGHT - THE VARIOUS STATES OF HUMAN BEINGS   138
THE DISTINCT FEATURES OF DISOBEDIENCE AND THE RIGHTEOUS PATH   138
1. THE ASPECT OF ANIMAL NATURE AND SATISFYING THE LUST   138
2. REQUIREMENTS OF THE NATURE   141
3. THE CATEGORY OF THE PEOPLE OF COMPULSION (COERCION)   141
4. THE ASPECT OF DIVINE DECREE   142
5. THE WISDOM   142
6. TAWHID OR ONENESS OF ALLAH   145
7. THE DIVINE NAMES AND ATTRIBUTES OF ALLAH   148
8. SUPPORT AND DESERTION   152
9. INCREASE IN FAITH AND ITS EVIDENCE   155
10. THE SITUATION OF MERCY   158
11. THE CONDITION OF WEAKNESS AND INCAPACITY   159
12. THE POSITION OF HUMBLENESS AND SUBMISSION   160
13. THE SCENE OF DEVOTION, LOVE AND DESIRE TO MEET ALLAH   162

INDEX   164

FOREWORD

Tawbah, to return to Allah in repentance is a gift by Allah to His worshippers. Through it, the Almighty forgives and wipes out the misdeeds of wrongdoers. Human beings are weak, as the Holy Qur'an has affirmed. Every human is susceptible to make mistakes. The Qur'an asks the believers not to be subject of frustration but rather gives them hope. It teaches them to ask Allah to take care of them and guide them to the right path. Tawbah in various forms has been cited more than 80 times in the Holy Qur'an. One of the beautiful names of Allah the Exalted is *Tawwab* i.e. the One who responds to the supplication of the worshipper and grants him forgiveness when he returns to Him in repentance.

True repentance consists of remorse, refraining from committing the mistake again and praying to the Most Merciful to forgive. One of the conditions of the repentance is that the person should behave in a correct manner, always be conscious of Allah, and let his heart be humble and full of contrition.

The book in your hand is composed in a Sufi style and deals with spiritual side of tawbah without neglecting the physical requirement and conditions. Its title, "Madarij Al-Salikin Bayn Manazil Iyyaka Na'budu Wa Iyyak Nasta'in" (*The Stages of the Travellers Between the Stations of Only You We Worship and Only You We Seek Help From*) gives an idea about its content. The author is the famous scholar Ibn Qayyim Al-Jawziyyah, Muhammad ibn Abu Bakr ibn Ayyub (1292-1350 CE).

This book is in fact a commentary on another treatise, "Manazil Al-Sa'irin" by Shaikh Abdullah Al-Hirawi (1006-1089 CE), a famous Sufi and theologian. This work deals with the stations of Sufism. The treatise is a short one, approximately 140 pages, written in a poetic language. He divided the stations to 100 in 10 main sections. The station of repentance is explained in three pages only. However, because of its importance, Ibn Al-Qayyim expanded it into more than 200 pages. Many statements of the Shaikh were very ambiguous and some of them gave the wrong impression. The author of *Madarij* did his best to explain all the concepts, but failed to explain some of them. Both are trying to explain the *maqamat* (stations) that a seeker of the spiritual purification wants to acquire. They use terms of the Sufism such as *sayr, manzil, salik* etc. However, Ibn Al-Qayyim tried to relate everything with the Qur'an and especially with the opening chapter (al-Fatihah). He believes that this chapter contains all the components of *'ubudiyyah* (devotion to Allah), which Sufis are looking for.

Ibn Al-Qayyim wrote a number of book on various subjects. This is one of his best works. In it, the author deals with apparent and deeper aspects of repentance. Some of the issues he discusses are:

i. The conditions of the repentance

ii. Whether repentance is required immediately

iii. If repentance from one sin is valid if the person insists on committing another one

iv. Whether a person can return to the same position he held after repentance

v. Whether a man who committed a sin and repented can reach the status of the one who is free from any sin

vi. What the conditions of 'sincere repentance' (*Tawbatan Nasuh*) are, which the Qur'an commands the believers to perform?

vii. Whether it is a requirement of the validity of repentance that the person should not commit the sin again

Ibn Al-Qayyim, based on his profound depth of knowledge, asserted that Allah Almighty has divided people into two categories: those who turn to Him in repentance and those who are wrongdoers. There is no third category.

There are other topics related to the subject which he explains, such as major and minor sins, difference of opinions of the scholars in the definition and number of major sins, difference between forgiveness and removing of the sin (*maghfirah* and *takfir*) and the causes which compel a person to commit a sin.

At very beginning, the author says that the repentance is the first of the stations, its middle and the last one. He has dealt with 100 stations of the travellers to come closer to Allah and achieve His pleasure. Throughout his discussion he quotes verses from the Qur'an and the sayings of the Messenger, may Allah's blessing and peace be upon him.

He deals with the true essence of repentance and its conditions. He shows its importance and quotes authentic sayings of the Messenger of Allah about it.

He quoted a statement from the Messenger in which he said that Allah feels happier by the repentance of His worshipper than a traveller in desert who lost his camel with all his provisions. He searched but could not trace it, lost hope and lay under the shade of a tree and slept. When he opened his eyes he found his camel standing before him with all his belongings. He was overwhelmed by the joy and said in ecstasy: 'O Allah, You are my slave and I am Your Lord'. He made a mistake in his excitement. *(Muslim)*

A good portion of the book is devoted to the discussion of theological questions like whether good and bad can be known by reason, and the dispute about the Attributes of Allah among the different sects. Most of these discussions have not been translated because of their complicated nature and are of little or no use in our time.

The section occupies approximately 200 pages in original Arabic, but many subjects are dropped in translation. The reader will, I hope, enjoy reading the book and benefit from it. I have tried my best to convey the message in simple and lucid English.

I am grateful to my friend Dr. Zubair Chaudhry, a medical doctor, who despite being busy spared his valuable time to peruse the manuscript. He improved the language and enhanced the style. He also introduced chapter headings to keep readers engaged and remain focused on the profound topic of repentance. May Allah give him the best of rewards for his sincere efforts. Without his support and encouragement I may not have been able to complete the work.

I also acknowledge support and extend gratitude to my old friend Hafiz Abdul Waheed of Darussalam International Publications who encouraged me to accomplish the task of translation. May Allah reward him in the best way.

Abdul Ali Hamid

Slough, Berks, SL1 3PP
E-mail: aahamid@hotmail.com

CHAPTER ONE
FUNDAMENTALS OF REPENTANCE (TAWBAH)

SIGNIFICANCE OF REPENTANCE

The station of repentance is the first stage of the servant's journey and it is the middle and the last one as well. The traveller does not part with it. He continues with it until the last moment of his life. If he moves from it to another stage, he carries and sticks with it. Repentance is the beginning and the end of the servant. He needs it inevitably at the end as he needs it at the beginning. Allah the Glorious said:

"Turn to Allah together O believers in repentance so that you may prosper." *(24:31)*

This verse belongs to the Madinan period in which Allah addressed the people of faith and the best of His creatures to turn to Him in repentance after they believed, showed patience, emigrated and engaged in jihad. He attached prosperity with repentance like the cause and effect. He used the word "la'alla" (may) which indicates expectation, to point out that when you turn in repentance, you will hope for success because the hope of success belongs only to those who turn to Allah in repentance. May Allah make us among those!

Allah also said:

"Those who do not repent are evildoers." *(49:11)*

The Almighty divided the servants into repentant and evildoer. There is no third category and He called the person who did not repent an evildoer. This was because he was the biggest evildoer as he failed to acknowledge his Lord and His rights, and was not aware of his faults and the bad consequences of his deeds.

It is reported in the authentic collection of Hadith that the Messenger of Allah ﷺ said, "People, turn to Allah in repentance. By Allah, I certainly turn to Him in repentance more than seventy times in a day."

His Companions counted him saying a hundred times in one sitting, "My Lord, forgive me and turn to me in mercy, You are the Ever Relenting, the Most Forgiving."

After the chapter (110) "When the help of Allah and the victory comes" was revealed he did not miss saying in his prayer, "Glory be to You, our Lord, and praise be to You. O Allah, forgive me."

It is also reported through authentic means that he said, "No one can be saved by his deeds."

His Companions asked, "Even you. O messenger of Allah?"
He replied, "Even me, unless Allah covers me with His mercy."

May Allah's blessings and peace be on the one who was most knowledgeable of Allah and His rights, His greatness and the humbleness deserved by His majesty, and the one who was most aware of the submission to Him and its requirements and the most regular in carrying them out.

REPENTANCE COMES WITH THE GUIDANCE OF ALLAH

The real essence of repentance is that the servant returns to Allah and leaves the path of those who have earned the wrath of Allah and those who have gone astray. This cannot be achieved except with the guidance of the Almighty to the straight path. Allah's guidance cannot be procured without His help and acknowledgement of His unity. The opening chapter has contained these matters beautifully and indicated them most perfectly. If a person gives this chapter its due in understanding, realising, visualising and comprehending its content, he will know for sure that its reading must be done with more sincere repentance. It is because the thorough and full guidance to the straight path cannot be gained with the ignorance of the sins or with persistence on committing them. The ignorance is incompatible with the recognition of the guidance, and persistence is transgression which is in contradiction with his intention. For this reason the repentance will not be correct unless the sin is recognised and acknowledged, and escaping from its bad consequences is sought for altogether.

The servant is required to look at three matters regarding the sin: being stripped from the shelter when he committed it, feeling happy while doing it and showing indifference from making amends while he knows for sure that Allah, the Truth, is watching him. If he is deprived of the protection of Allah, it means that he has neglected taking resort to Him. If he had resorted to Allah, he would not have gone out of the guidance of obedience. Allah, the Most Glorious, said:
"Whosoever holds fast to Allah will be guided to the straight path." *(3:101)*

If his reliance on Allah was complete He would have not deserted him. He, the Most High, said:
"Hold fast to Allah. He is your protector, an Excellent Protector and an Excellent Helper."
(22:78)

The verse means that if you hold fast to Allah, He will give you protection and help you against your soul and against Satan. They are the two enemies which never leave the side of the servant. Their enmity is more harmful that the enmity of any person from outside.

To get support against this enemy is very important and the servant is in need of it. However, the full support against the enemy will be in accordance with the degree of holding fast to Allah.

Being removed from the shelter of Allah may also apply to the case where a servant commits a sin after turning in repentance to Allah. When he realises that he has been deprived of the protection and knows the devastating result of it, he will be aware of its significance and be sure that he is going to be destroyed. This is the real desertion. Allah did not leave him to commit the sin but he committed the sin after He deserted him and left him alone. If Allah had given him protection and guidance, the sin would not have been able to reach him.

The people who know Allah properly say that desertion is that Allah leaves you to yourself and makes your soul dominate you. The support is that He does not leave you to your soul. In all these procedures He has wisdom and secrets known only to Him.

Feeling happy with the sin is an evidence of intense desire of it. It also shows unconsciousness of the status of the one who has been disobeyed, and ignorance of the seriousness of its consequences. All this was covered from him by his happiness, which is more harmful to him than the mere commitment of the sin. A believer can never be happy with disobedience of Allah and can never enjoy it. When he happens to commit it, his heart feels sorrow and pain. However, the intoxication of desire prevents him from sensing it. If a person's heart is free from this sorrow, and his happiness and joy are strong then he should examine his faith and cry over the death of his heart. If his heart was alive, it would have make him sad with the commitment of the sin, create anger in him and he would find it difficult to sustain it. But if the heart has lost feeling, then it is dead and there is no chance that the person will feel the guilt. This point concerning the sin is known only to a very few people, though it is very dangerous and can lead to destruction if not checked by three things: (a) fear of death before repentance, (b) regret over what was missed by the violation of the command of Allah and (c) work hard to redress it.

To persist in the disregard of the commands of Allah and the determination to continue is another sin. It is actually more serious than the first sin. It is the punishment of the sinful person that he is driven to commit another sin, followed by another, until his total loss is completed.

To persist in committing sins is another sin and to show indifference in redressing the disobedience is persistence, which is the sign of annihilation. More dangerous than this is to commit offences openly while being sure that the Lord of the might and glory is watching him from above His throne. If he believes that Allah is watching over him and yet he continues to do it openly, then that is a very serious matter. If he does not believe in Allah watching and being aware of his act, he is a disbeliever and out of Islam altogether. He is moving between two things: lack of shame and openly disregarding the witnessing of Allah and disbelief and casting off religion. Therefore it is necessary to make repentance with certainty that the servant is sure that Allah is watching him and is aware of his acts. He observes him overtly when he commits a sin. This form of repentance is not appropriate for anyone except a Muslim. If a person is not convinced of the witnessing of Allah over him and denies it, then his repentance is to embrace Islam and affirm the Attributes of Allah, the Lord of Might.

THE CONDITIONS OF REPENTANCE

The conditions of repentance are three:
a) to regret
b) to desist and
c) to apologise

The essence of repentance is to regret what was committed in the past, to abstain from it immediately and make a firm resolution not to commit it again in future. All three conditions must be found at the time of repentance. The servant should show regret, refrain from the sin and make a firm resolution not to return to it. When he attains this he returns to position of servitude for which he has been created. This coming back is the essence of the repentance.

Since the repentance was dependant on the above three matters, they were designated as conditions for it. Without regret, repentance will not be realised. If a person does not lament over the bad act, it means that he is pleased with it and will repeat it. The Prophet ﷺ said, "Regret is repentance."

As far as desistance is concerned, repentance cannot be realised with committing the sin. As for the apology, it is problematic. Some people say that the perfectness of the repentance is not to apologise because the apology is to argue about the crime, and abandoning it to acknowledge it, and the repentance cannot be valid without acknowledgement. It is proved by the following lines said by a poet to his boss who had reproved him on something, "I do not counter your rebuke by apology but say as you say, 'I knock the door of your pardon with humility, and kind behaviour will decide between us.'"

When the boss heard his words he stood up immediately, approached him then removed his anger towards him. So the perfect acknowledgement requires refraining from apology. The heart and the tongue should be saying, "My Lord, I have no excuse for the sin so that I can apologise and have no power to gain victory, I am a sinner asking for forgiveness. My Lord, I have no excuse. It is Your absolute right and my fault. If You forgive me (it will be good) otherwise You have full right."

The apology here is to show weakness and humility as well as the domination of the enemy and the power of the soul. It is to admit that what was done was not because of undervaluing Allah's right or having no knowledge of it. Nor it was a result of denying Allah's awareness or taking His threat lightly. It was the result of the domination of the desire and the weakness of the power to resist the illness of the desire. It was also due to expecting His forgiveness, hoping for His generosity and aspiring for the vastness of His forbearance and mercy. The chief deceiver, i.e. Satan, deceived you. You were tempted by the evil commanding your soul and Allah's cover that was spread over you. Your ignorance contributed towards this. Now there is no resort except to turn to Allah and seek His assistance. All such words are to be said to seek Allah's favour, to show the humility and poverty and to admit the inability and to acknowledge the full submission.

This is an element of the perfection of the repentance adopted by clever people who flatter their Lord Almighty, and Allah loves His servant to show flattery to Him. It is said in a Hadith: "Flatter Allah."

It is reported through authentic chain that The Prophet, may Allah's blessing and peace be on him, said:
"No one loves excuses as Allah does."

Here it means to have an excuse as he said at the end of the Hadith:
"For that He sent the messengers with good tidings and warnings."

Allah, the Most High, said:
"Delivering a reminder as a proof or a warning." (77:5-6)

It is a part of Allah Almighty's perfect justice and kindness that He offered excuse to His servants. He does not hold the unjust people unless He has fully offered excuses and established the evidence. He loves His servant to apologise to Him and withdraw from his sin. According to an authentic Hadith, the Messenger of Allah 襟 said:
"Whoever offers an apology to Allah, He accepts his apology."

This is the praiseworthy and useful apology.

To make excuses on the basis of Divine decree is to dispute with Allah, glory be to Him. It is an objection by the servant against the Lord and attributing his mistake to the destiny. This was the way of the enemies of Allah as was said by some of their leaders concerning the following Qur'anic verse:
"The love of desirable things is made alluring for men – women, children, gold and silver treasures piled up high, horses with fine marking, livestock, and farmland" (3:14)
He asked his followers:

"Do you know what is meant by this verse?"

They asked him, "What is meant?"

He replied that it was to establish the excuses of the creature.

This person is ignorant of Allah and His speech, and gave a false interpretation. The message of the verse is to arouse a dislike for the transitory and vanishing materials, and to induce interest in that which is permanent and everlasting. It is also derogatory for the one who prefers that alluring thing and goes after it. He is like a child who is given something interesting to play with - he feels happy with it and is attracted to it. In the verse, the subject of "making alluring" is not mentioned. Allah did not say that "We made alluring for men". The Lord Almighty assigns allurement of the world and the sins to Satan. He said:

"And Satan made their foul deeds alluring to them." *(6:43)*

"In the same way, their idols have induced many of the pagans to kill their own children." *(6:137)*

In the Hadith the Messenger ﷺ said, "I have been sent as a guide and caller but I have no power to guide, on the other hand the Devil has been sent as misguiding and making things alluring but he has no power to misguide either."

It is in no way in contradiction to the following statement of Allah:

"To each community We make their own actions seem alluring." *(6:108)*

The attribution of allurement to Him is as the decree and to Satan as the cause. Allah's work in making things alluring to them is a kind of punishment for their inclination to what Satan has made alluring to them. The punishment of a bad deed is a bad deed as the reward of a good deed is a good deed after it.

The point is that the excuse on the basis of the decree is in contradiction to repentance and has nothing to do with apology.

There is a saying that when a servant commits a sin and says. "My Lord, it was Your decree. You gave me power over it, You decided it for me and You wrote it for me," Allah, the Most High says, "You did it, you executed it and you willed it and made effort for it. I am going to punish you for that."

But if the servant says, "My Lord, I did wrong, made mistake and transgressed. I did it myself," Allah the Mighty says, "I decided and decreed it for you and I wrote it for you, but now I forgive you."

When a person does a good deed and says, "My Lord, I did it, I gave in charity, I performed prayer and I fed the poor," Allah says, "I helped you and gave you support in doing it."

If the servant says, "My Lord, You gave me help and support and You showed favour to me," Allah says: 'But you did it and you willed it and you executed it.'

Apology is of two kinds:
a) An apology that is in contradiction with acknowledgement, therefore that is contradictory to repentance and
b) An apology that is based on acknowledgement. This is part of the perfection of repentance.

THE ESSENTIAL COMPONENTS OF REPENTANCE

The essence of repentance is composed of three matters:
a) To regard the crime (wrongdoing) as significant
b) To reproach the repentance and
c) To seek the apology of the people affected

The essence is explained as the most important and distinctive feature of something, that which determines its identity and which also ascertains the existence and correctness of it.

The Prophet ﷺ said to Harithah, "Every truth has an essence, so what is the essence of your faith?"

Regarding the crime as significant is essential because if he considers it little, he will not feel regret. The regret of a person would be according to the seriousness of his crime when committed. If a person considers losing a penny as insignificant, he will not be regretful for this loss, but when he knows that it is a dinar, he will be more regretful and its loss will cause him much anguish.

Regarding the crime as big ensues from three factors:
a) Giving importance to the command
b) Glorification of the Master and
c) Being sure of the requital

Reproaching the repentance is a duty for him because he does not know for sure that he has fulfilled his due to the way it was required. He should fear that he has not done it properly and it has not been accepted from him because he did not make effort to do it appropriately. He should feel that his repentance was for a need, such as the repentance of the people in need and poverty who wish to get their needs fulfilled and their ranks among the people preserved.

He thinks that his repentance was to protect his (overburdening) condition and it was not for the fear of the Lord of Might, or he repented for reasons unjustified, such as:
• The purpose of seeking comfort from the exertion in committing the sin or
• For the fear of damage to his honour, his wealth or his rank, or
• For the weakness of the motive of disobedience in his heart
• Dying out of the fire of desire or
• Inconsistency of the sin with his request of knowledge, provision etc.

Aforementioned are the causes that make repentance not offered for the fear of Allah, asserting His greatness, showing respect to His sacred ordinances, revering Him and being afraid of losing the status with Him, being driven from Him and being kept away from looking at His Face in the Hereafter. This repentance is one thing and the repentance of the people of excuses is something else.

A person may discredit his repentance for the weakness of his intention and the remembrance of the sin from time to time and enjoy the memory of its doing. He may breathe a sigh of relief or feel in commotion.

It is also a discredit to the repentance that the man feels content and confident that he has turned in repentance as though he has been given an assurance of safety. This contentment is a source of damage to the repentance.

Another sign is the stagnation of the eye, continuation of indifference and negligence of good deeds which he did not do before the sin.

The correct and satisfactory repentance has distinguishing marks. Among them is that the person becomes better than he was before repentance. Another mark is that he is always scared and never feels secure from the scheme of Allah. His fear remains with him until the time he hears the saying of those who come to take his soul:
"Have no fear or grief, but rejoice in the good news of Paradise, which you have been promised." (41:30)

When he hears these words, his fear departs.

Another sign is the breaking down of his heart into pieces out of regret and fear. This depends on the degree of the gravity of the crime. Allah, the Most High, said:
"The building they have founded will always be a source of doubt within their hearts, until their hearts are cut to pieces." (9:110)

Ibn Uyaynah commented on it by saying that the hearts will be cut in pieces by repentance.

There is no doubt that intense fear of severe torment leads to the cracking and splitting of the heart. This is what is meant by cutting in pieces in the verse, and it is the essence of repentance. For the man whose repentance is proper, his heart breaks down in regret for his negligence and fear of bad consequences. A person whose heart does not experience this pain for the negligence he committed in this world and does not feel regret and fear, his heart will be torn asunder in the Hereafter when the truth will be exposed and he will witness the reward of the obedient and the torment of the disobedient ones. The heart has to be torn asunder either in this world or in the Hereafter.

One of the prerequisites of correct repentance is a special dejection of the heart, which is incomparable to anything. It occurs to the sinner only. It is not produced by hunger or the spiritual exercise of mere love. It is something beyond all these matters. It cleaves the heart completely before the Lord Almighty, surrounding him from every side and throwing him before his Lord, dumped, humiliated and submissive. His condition is like a slave who committed a crime and ran away from his master. He was captured and presented before his master having no one to save him. He had no escape from him nor can he ignore him or expect deliverance from him. He knows for sure that his life, happiness, success and prosperity lie in his master's pleasure with him. He is aware that his master has comprehensive knowledge of his faults. Nevertheless, he loves his master very much and needs him all the time. He is also aware of his weakness and inability, and the power and might of his master.

All these conditions produce humility, diffidence and self-abasement, which are very useful to the servant. They are the greatest source of strength and the surest means of bringing him closer to his master. There is nothing dearer to his master than humbleness, submissiveness, obedience and self-surrender to him. He can say in that condition, "By your power and my inability, I beg you to have mercy on me. I entreat you by your power and my weakness, and by your independence from me and my need of you. This is my untruthful forehead before you. You have many slaves beside me, but I have you only as my master. There is no place of refuge and safety but to you. I am begging you like a poor person and praying earnestly like a humble and abased person. I implore you like a blind and scared man, like a person whose neck has surrendered to you, his head lowered, his eyes filled with tears and his heart disgraced."

This type of feeling is the indication of accepted repentance. If a person does not have such feeling, he should blame his repentance and try to amend it. The real repentance is very hard, but very easy by tongue and pretension. A true person does not experience anything more difficult than sincere and true repentance. There is no power or strength except with Allah.
Most of the people who avoid obvious grave sins are involved in similar sins or greater or smaller than them. It never occurs to their minds that what they do are sins which require repentance. They despise those who commit grave sins and feel proud of their good deeds. They show happiness by their behaviour and expect people to praise them on their pious

deeds. The consequences of their acts are more hateful to Allah than the grave sins of those people.

If Allah Almighty causes one of them to commit a grave sin in order to make him humble and take the arrogance of pious deeds from his heart, it is a mercy for him. It is similar to His mercy towards the people of the grave sins who turn to Him with sincere repentance and submissive hearts. It is a mercy for them. Otherwise both are in danger.

CHAPTER TWO
UNDERSTANDING THE DECREE OF ALLAH

MAKING EXCUSES FOR SINS

Regarding seeking an apology from people, there are two ways: one is good and the other is bad and prohibited.

The bad one is to seek an apology concerning the Divine decree, which they cannot escape. This idea is very dangerous and without much benefit. If someone absolves the enemies of Allah and those who disobey Him and His Messengers from any guilt and tries to justify their acts, he is violating the command of Allah. He endeavours to find excuse for someone whom Allah has not excused. He has blamed him and commanded to blame him. It is not consistent with Allah's wish. Rather, to disparage such a person is what Allah prefers. The Almighty has removed all excuses from him. If this man had any excuse, Allah would not have punished him. The Most Merciful is the Most Beneficent, Just and free from punishing a man who has an excuse. No one appreciates excuses more than Allah, the Most Forgiving. He sent the Messengers and revealed the Books so that mankind would have no excuse before Him.

Now a man who is trying to establish an excuse for such people who do not follow the commands of Allah is trying to provide ground for justification, which Allah has nullified completely. The people who have real excuses, such as a child who does not have the ability of discernment, or an insane person, or a person whom the call of Islam did not reach, or a deaf and blind person who is unable to see and hear – Allah will not punish them for no reason. He has set a separate judgment for them on the Day of Judgement. He will put them to test by sending a messenger to them. The one who obeys the messenger, will be admitted in Paradise, and the one who disobeys him will go to Hell. There are reports from the Messenger of Allah, ﷺ to this effect.

If someone raises a question on these reports and argues that they are not in conformity with the reason because the Hereafter is the abode of requital and not of commandments, he is ignorant. He should be aware that responsibility will end with the entrance in Paradise or Hell. It will continue in the *Barzakh* (an intermediate state between after death and before resurrection) and on the arena of the Judgement. It is supported by the fact that Allah will call the people to prostrate to Him. The believers will do it willingly and the disbelievers and the hypocrites will not be able to prostrate.

The point is that no one has an excuse for disobeying Allah's commands, when he has knowledge of them and is free to abide or to neglect. If people were to have excuses to disobey Allah, they would not have deserved punishment and reprimand in this word or in the next one. One can say that your argument is on the basis of the Shari'ah. If you look at the people from the perspective of the reality, you will excuse them. Undoubtedly they are moving in accordance with Allah's Decree about them. They are targets of the arrows of the Divine Decree. You are judging them on the basis of the Shari'ah, but we are looking at them from the angle of the Decree. Both of us have a point in this regard.

The answer to this argument is that if the excuse is not acceptable, it is of no use. Resorting to the Decree is unacceptable. Nobody is to be excused by it. What you said was false and useless. It will rather aggravate his crime and Allah will get angry with him. No sensible person can argue in this way.

Taking cover in the Divine Decree means to clear the side of the offender while he is unjust and ignorant. Such people are the opponents of Allah. They have various complaints and forceful petitions. If they look thoroughly in the corners of their hearts, they will find another opponent there, who is full of complaint. He says, "I cannot say anything; I am wronged in the form of wrongdoer." He says in agony, "Poor the son of Adam! Neither has he power nor is he excused."

Another man says, "The son of Adam is a ball under the bats of the Decree, one person hits it from one side and the other returns from the other. Can the ball get justice from the bats?" Anyone with even the least understanding will realise that all this is simply complaining and moaning. If he looks carefully at his soul, he will find the source of all evils in it. This is the utmost degree of ignorance and injustice. Allah has said about the man:
"He (man) is unjust and ignorant." *(33:72)* while **"Allah is Free of need and Praiseworthy."** *(35:15)*

This unjust and ignorant man should know that all his trouble and problem emanate from him, and he deserved every blame and reprimand.

"Indeed man is ungrateful to his Lord." *(100:6)*

If this ignorant and unjust man only knew that he is sitting on the path of his interests, but he is blocking himself from reaching them! He is the stone obstructing the way of water on which his life depends. He has blocked the flow of the water to the garden of his heart and cries, "thirst, thirst!" He is covering his heart from the secrets of the unseen, and he is the cloud that obstructs the shining of the sun on the heart. There is nothing more harmful to him than himself and no one more damaging than him alone. The enemies cannot cause so much harm to an ignorant as he causes to himself. May he perish! He is a wrongdoer but tries to appear in the form of being wronged. He complains but he is the cause of the offence. He earnestly turns away and cries, "They have expelled me and drove me away." He turned back from the door, and rather closed it on himself and lost its keys. Yet he claims, "He called me and shut the door in my face. Is there any way for me to enter?"

The Kind one is holding him from the Fire, but he struggles to free himself, loses control and plunges into it. Then calls for help saying, "What can I do? They pulled me to the ditch and threw me in it."

A sincere advisor cautioned him, "Be aware, keep away." He held him by his clothes and showed him the horrible conditions of those who were there, yet he was adamant to enter it.

Woe to him! He is the supporter of Satan against his Lord and enemy of Allah for his soul. He commits sinful acts, thinking that he has no power to resist and keeps away from good deeds by his own will. He has no willpower and loses all his chances. He neglects his interests and blames the Decree of his Lord.

He argues with Allah in a way which he would not accept from his slave or his wife if they were to complain about the negligence of some of his duties. If he asked one of them to do something and they neglected to do so, or he orders them to keep away from something and yet they don't, then they say the Decree pushed them to it, we would not accept this excuse and would immediately punish them.

One can ask this ignorant and unjust man: 'If an excuse is correct in abandoning the right of your Lord, why is it not for your slave or maid for abandoning some of your rights?' If a person behaves badly to you or commits a crime against you and takes refuge in the Decree, you would be very angry with him. His crime will be more serious to you and you will find his excuse invalid. But here you use this excuse against your Lord and feel that it is enough! Who, then, is closer to ignorance and injustice?

This is your behaviour while the Allah's favour is surrounding you throughout your life. He, glory is to Him, removed all your excuses, granted you the opportunity to work for His Paradise and guided you. He supplied you with the provisions for your journey and equipped you with means of combating the highway robbers. He, by His grace, gave you hearing and sight and mind, made you able to recognise good and bad, useful and harmful. He sent His Messenger to you, sent down His Book to you, and gave you the power to remind, and to understand and to practice. The Almighty provided you with His noble soldiers from amongst the angels, who support you and protect you. They fight your enemy and repel him from you. They want you not to incline to the enemy or make compromises with him when they are engaged in your defence. But you insist on helping him against them and befriending him besides them. You join him and stand by him, leaving your true friend aside, who should have been taken as a friend by you. Allah said in the Qur'an:

"We said to the angels: 'Bow down before Adam,' and they all bowed down, but not Iblis (the devil). He was one of the jinn and he disobeyed his Lord's command. Are you (people) going to take him and his offspring as your allies instead of Me, even though they are your enemies? What a bad exchange for the evildoers." *(18:50)*

He expelled Iblis from the heaven and drove him away from His Garden and banned him from approaching Him. He, the Lord, did this because the devil did not prostrate to Adam. Allah declared the devil as His enemy and kicked him out, but you sympathise with him and befriend him, and yet you complain and grumble about being driven away. You say, "they made me used to union, and union is sweet, but they afflicted me with rejection, and the rejection is hard."

Why should not a man who behaves like this be driven away and banished? How can a person who has spoiled his relations with Allah be made among the people of distinction and close friends of Him?

Allah commanded him to give thanks to Him, not because He was in need of it, but rather to increase His favour upon him. But he was ungrateful of His bounties and used them in matters leading to His anger. This resulted in diverting His favour from him.

He, the Most High, commanded him to remember Him and remember His grace, but he forgot Him and the result was that Allah forgot him as He said:
"They forgot Allah, so He made them forget themselves." *(59:19)*

"They forgot Allah, so He forgot them." *(9:67)*

He ordered him to implore Him so that He can give to him, but he did not. Yet, He granted him the greatest bounties without asking, but he did not accept them. He complained against the One who showed mercy to him, to the one who is unable to help him. He grumbled against the One who does not do injustice. If He favoured him with health, well being, wealth and position, he used them in His disobedience. If He took them away from him, he became unhappy from his Lord and complained. His response was incorrect in both prosperity and adversity. Prosperity pushed him to do things that caused Allah's anger and adversity pushed him to deny His favour and show ungratefulness, and complain against Him to His creatures.

He, the Most Generous, called him to His door, but he did not heed nor did he knock at it. When He opened it for him, he did not enter. The Most Merciful sent His Messenger to him, who called him to the abode of his honour, but he disobeyed the Messenger and said: 'I am not going to sell the present for the absent. I will not abandon what I have for what I only hear about.' If he saw the benefit in obeying the Messenger, he would follow him for the expected benefit, not for the pleasure of the One who has sent him. In this way he continued in his sinful acts until Allah turned away from him and closed His door in his face.

In spite of all that Allah did not deprive him of the hope, but said:
'Whenever you come to Me I will welcome you. If you come in the night I will be ready to receive you; if you come in daytime I will welcome you. If you approach Me a span of the hand I will come to you the length of an arm. If you come near Me the length of an arm I will come closer the length of outstretched arms. If you walk to Me, I will come running to you. If you come to Me with an full of earth of sins, but have not associated partners to Me, I will meet you with similar amount of forgiveness. If your sins reach the height of the heavens and you seek forgiveness, I will forgive you. Who is, then, more generous and benevolent than Me?'

The Almighty then says, "My servants combat Me with grave sins, yet I guard them on their beds. I and man and jinn are engaged in a momentous contest. I create, but someone else is worshipped. I give provision, but others are thanked. My good is coming down to My servants and their evil deeds are ascending to Me. I endear Myself to them by My favours while I have no need of them, but they make Me angry with sins while they are in dire need of Me. Whoever comes to Me I meet him from afar, whoever turns away from Me I call him from nearby. Those who obey Me deserve My honour; however those who disobey Me I do not make them lose hope of My mercy. If they turn to Me in repentance, I am their beloved. I love those who turn to Me in repentance and those who struggle to keep clean. Nevertheless if they do not turn to Me I am their healer. I cause them suffering so that I can cleanse them from faults. Anyone who puts Me over others, I prefer him over others. Good deeds are compensated by Me ten times more to seven hundred times to many times more. The sin is repaid by Me with its equal, and if the man regrets and asks Me for forgiveness, I forgive him. I appreciate little deeds and forgive many mistakes. My mercy dominated My anger. My forbearance is above My censure and My pardon is above My punishment. I am more compassionate to My servants than a mother to her child."

The Messenger ﷺ said, "Certainly Allah is happier from the repentance of His servant than a man who has lost his camel, which had his food and drink on it, in a dangerous desert. He searched for it till he lost his hope of finding it and slept below a tree waiting for death. He woke up and found his camel standing near him, its noseband attached to the tree. Allah is happier with the repentance of His servant than this man is from seeing his camel."

This is the happiness of benevolence, kindness and compassion, and not the happiness of being in need of His servant's repentance and expecting some benefit out of it. Similarly His affinity of His servant is to show love, kindness and affection to him. It is not for the aim of increasing the number of His supporters or getting out of humbleness to honour. He is not in need of getting help against others or taking him as refuge for hardship. He said:

"Say; Praise belongs to Allah, who has neither child nor partner in His rule. He is not so weak as to need a protector. Proclaim His limitless greatness." *(17:111)*

He denied having a protector from weakness, He on the other hand is the protector of those who believe, and they are His allies. This is the case of the Lord and the servant. They are trying to establish their excuses and refer their faults to the Decree.

This is one of the two meanings of the statement that the reality of repentance is to seek excuses for the creature. It should have been made clear to you that seeking excuses for people for their offences is damaging repentance.

REFERRING THE MATTERS TO THE DECREE OF ALLAH

The second meaning is to establish their excuse in treating you badly and causing you harm. You look in this matter to the Decree and feel that their deeds are like the movements of the trees. In this way you refer to the Decree regarding your right not the right of your Lord. This explanation is true. However, it is the status of the great devotees and close friends of Allah. One of them ignores their rights, but fulfils the right of his Lord perfectly. He looks in the negligence and violation of his right at the Decree, but considers the command regarding the right of Allah. He seeks excuse for abuse of his right, but he is not ready to accept it in the right of Allah. This was the condition of our Prophet ﷺ as 'A'ishah ◈ said, "Never did the messenger of Allah ﷺ take revenge for himself. It never happened that a wrong was done to him and he retaliated, unless the orders of Allah were violated. In that case nothing could appease his anger until he took revenge for the sake of Allah".

'A'ishah ◈ also said, "Never did the Messenger of Allah ﷺ hit a servant or an animal or anything with his hand, except in the case of jihad in Allah's cause".

Anas ◈ related, "I served the Messenger of Allah ﷺ for ten years and he never asked me about something which I did, 'Why did you do it?' Or about something which I did not do, 'Why did you not do it?' When some members of his family rebuked me, he would say, 'Leave him. If something was decreed it would have taken place."

Consider his reference to the Decree when the matter was regarding right or wrong. He cut the hand of the woman when Allah's right was concerned and did not say that it was the Decree. The same is true about his intention of burning the people who lagged behind when attending prayer with him. He did not say, "If the prayer was decreed for them they would have done it." The same thing can be said in his action of stoning to death a man and a woman when they committed adultery. He did not refer to the Decree. His act concerning the people of Uraynah who murdered his keeper and drove away the camels and renounced Islam is another example. He did not say that it was the Decree, but ordered their feet and hands to be amputated alternately, for their eyes to be teared out, and for them to be left in the stony area. They asked for water but it was not given to them until they died of thirst. There are many other examples.

The messenger of Allah ﷺ perfectly knew Allah and His right, and did not resort to the Decree in any case of violation of His commands.

This second explanation, though it might make sense, is not among the requirements of repentance and it does not have any connection with it. It is not proper to seek excuses for the sins committed by a man. The reality of repentance is to display zeal for the command of Allah and show anger against violating it. It is much better than seeking excuses for the violation of His commands and prohibitions. If excuses are allowed then the worshippers of idols and images and the murderers of the prophets will use it. Pharaoh, Haman, Nimrod, Abu Jahl and his allies, Satan and his soldiers and every disbeliever and wrongdoer and transgressor of the limits ordained by Allah and those involved in violation of His commands will put forward their excuses that all of them are under the Decree. Will it be right to consider their excuses as the part of the reality of repentance?

How can one forward the excuse of someone to his beloved when he is not willing to accept it? He is extremely angry with him, has driven him away from his door and despises him intensely. If someone accepts his excuses, he is subjecting himself for the anger of the beloved and lowering his position to him.

The attempt to understand Allah's Decrees is like an example of the sea, on which is a ship that moves in waves as huge as mountains. People come to the shore and wish to board the ship. One man stands there in astonishment, unable to move, his heart filled with the greatness of what he is witnessing. He decides to stand on the shore, thinking it unwise to put himself in danger. Another man, after hearing the raging of the sea and sound of its waves, turns away. He doesn't have courage to even look at it. A third person plunges in. He is taken down by a wave and brought up by another.

All three people are in danger. The one standing on the shore is at risk of the water reaching his feet. There is no safe haven for the one who runs away. The one who plunges in the waves witnesses people drowned at every moment. Only the fourth type of person is saved. This is the one who waited for the ship, and for its command. As it came closer, the captain called, "Board it, in the name of Allah is its course and anchorage." *(11:41)*

This is the ark of Nuh and the ark of the messengers who came after him. Whoever boarded was saved and anyone who stayed behind was drowned. They boarded the ark of command of Decree which sailed with them through the waves, and surrendered themselves to the Supreme Lord, who controls the seas. It was Lord's command to the earth and the heavens: **"Earth, swallow up your water, and sky, hold back (the rain)."** *(11:44)*

In the end the water subsided, and the command was fulfilled. The ark settled on Mount Judi, the mountain of rest. Those who stayed behind - such as the people of Nuh - were drowned and then burnt. It was announced to mankind:
"Away with the evildoers!" *(11:44)*

"We did not wrong them; they were the ones who did wrong." *(43:76)*

Then the terms of religion and the Decree for the confirmation of His Oneness and the establishment of His proof were announced:
"Say, the conclusive argument belongs to Allah alone. Had He so willed He would have guided you all." *(6:149)*

REALISATION OF THE DECREE OF ALLAH
The one who boarded this ark had to face the waves of the Decree and confront one by the other, otherwise he would perish. He confronts the Decree by another Decree. This is the way of the people of firm resolution among the pious ones. This is what the leading master of piety, Shaykh Abd al-Qadir al Gailani, said: "When the people arrive at the question of Decree, they stop, except me. An opening appears for me and I confront the decrees of the truth by the truth for the truth. The man is that who combats the Decree not the one who surrenders to the Decree".

If the affairs of the people in this life are not achieved without confronting the decree by one another, then how can it be possible concerning the Hereafter?

Allah, the Glorious, commanded us to repel evil, by His Decree, with the good deed - which is also by His Decree. Hunger is by His Decree, and He ordered us to treat it by eating, which is also by His Decree. If a person surrenders to the Decree of hunger while he is able to remove it by eating, and dies, he has committed a sin. The same applies to cold, heat and thirst. All these are by the Decree of Allah and He has commanded us to remove them by opposite means which are by His Decree as well.

This matter was explained by the prophet ﷺ very well in his statement when the Companions asked, "Messenger of Allah, what do you say about the medicines we use or the charm we apply, can they turn the Decree of Allah in any way?"

He replied, "They are parts of the Decree of Allah."

In another Hadith he said, "The supplication and the suffering combat with one another between the heavens and the earth."

When the disbelievers attack the land of the Muslims, they do it by the Decree of Allah. Is it then permissible for the Muslims to surrender to the Decree and refrain from defence? This is the Jihad which they have to engage in and thought it they are repelling the Decree of Allah by His Decree.

In the same way when a sin is decreed for you, you commit it by the Decree, now you must amend it through sincere repentance, which is also part of the Decree.

CONFRONTING THE DECREE BY THE DECREE

Repelling of the Decree by the Decree is of two kinds:

1. Repelling the Decree where the means of which are present, but it did not take place by other means of Decree, which obstruct its happening. For example, pushing away the enemy by fighting him, and removing the heat or cold, etc.

2. The second is to repel the Decree which has taken place by another Decree which removes it. This is like removing the Decree of illness by the Decree of taking medicine, and removing the Decree of the sin by the Decree of repentance, and repelling the Decree of bad behaviour by the Decree of good behaviour.

This is how the devoted servants of Allah act. They do not surrender to the Decrees and abandon working and using the means to combat them. They know that doing nothing is incapacity, which Allah the Most High does not like. When the servant is overwhelmed and has no power to challenge the Decree, he surrenders to it and becomes like a dead body in the hands of the washer who moves it the way he likes. In this case the annihilation in the Decree works, but when there is power to combat it then the useful annihilation is to dispense with the creature for the decision of Allah, to sacrifice one's desire for the command of Allah and prefer the will and love of Allah over his will and love. Such a person has indeed fulfilled the reality of:

"Only You we worship, and only You we turn for help." *(1:5)*

CHAPTER THREE
INNER DIMENSIONS OF REPENTANCE

SECRETS OF REPENTANCE

There are three secrets of the essence of repentance:
a) Caution against the glory
b) Disregard of the crime and
c) Repentance from repentance

The caution against the glory means that the objective of repentance is to attain consciousness of Allah. It requires the fear and awareness of Allah, and to carry out His commands and avoid His prohibition. The repentant person should engage in the deeds of obedience of the Almighty, hoping for the reward of Allah, and being afraid of His punishment. He does not have the sense of the glory of obedience. Obedience and repentance contain open and secret glory. So, the person's intention should not be an expression of glory, although he may be aware that it can be achieved by obedience and repentance. If a person repents for the sake of glory, his repentance is irregular. It is reported in some narration:
"Allah, the Glorious, inspired to one of the prophets that say to a certain pious man, 'By your indifference to the world you intended to get comfort, and by devoting yourself to Me you wanted glory. What did you do for Me?' The pious man asked: 'What remains for me to do for You after that, my Lord?' He replied: 'Did you take a friend for the sake of Me or take an enemy for the sake of Me?'"

The meaning of this is that comfort and glory were achieved by disregarding the world and through worship, but the fulfilment of Allah's due requires a person to make friends for His sake and take enemies for Him.

As for disregarding the crime, it has been explained in different manners. Some people have said that it requires ignoring the sin and disregarding it completely. It is better and more desirable for the repentant person to pass his time in Allah's remembrance with sincerity. It is said that the mention of estrangement in the moment of happiness is estrangement.

Some other people have said that it was better for him not to forget his fault, but to keep it constantly before his eyes. This will create humility and lowliness which are much better than the purity of his time. They have also said that this was why Dawud inscribed his mistake in his palm. He looked at it and cried. They also said: 'If you lose your way, return to your faults, you will find the way.'

The meaning of this is that when you return to your faults, you will be humble and low, and bow your head to Allah, as glory and honour belongs to Him. You will feel miserable and gloomy. This is the true path of servitude.

The case requires explanation. When a believer notices at the time of sincerity a cloud of claim and shade of arrogance and unawareness of the bounty, and his soul takes him away from the essence of his poverty and deficiency, then the remembrance of his faults is more desirable for him. But if he realises the favour of Allah to him, perceives his need to Him and understands that he is not free from His help at any moment, then forgetting his sin is better for him. He has reached a stage where his heart is overflowing with the love of Allah, he is pleased with Him, has desire to meet Him, and is able to witness His vast mercy, forbearance and forgiveness. His heart in illuminated with the lights of the beautiful Names and Attributes.

In such a situation if he remembers his faults, that condition will disappear from him. He will climb down from a high stage to a low one. The distance between the two stages is like the distance between the sky and the earth. This is the work of Satan who felt jealous of him and tried to bring him down from his stage and block his journey in the fields of love, affection and knowledge, and leave him deserted.

REPENTANCE FROM REPENTANCE

Repentance from repentance is an ambiguous statement which can give both true and false connotations. A person may speak it without distinction while his intention is right.

Repentance is the greatest good deed, and repentance from good deeds is the biggest sin and horrible transgression. As a matter of fact, it is disbelief if it is understood in its literal sense. There is no difference between repentance from repentance and repentance from Islam and belief. Will it be right, then, to speak of repentance from the belief?

However, it is intended to mean repentance from the vision of the repentance. The person must remember that he repented by the will and grace of Allah. If he was left to himself, he would have not been able to do it. When he starts looking at it and feels that he did it, and forgets the favour of Allah to him, he is required to repent from feeling and heedlessness. It is to be noted that this feeling and heedlessness are not the repentance, nor they are its components or conditions. It is another mistake which he has committed after the repentance. He is, therefore, required to repent from this mistake as he did from the first one. If, in all situations he repented from a sin, how can it be said that he repented from repentance?

It is an absurd and incorrect statement. It is possible that the repentance has a flaw, imperfection and defect which blocked its perfection. The person may be or may not be aware of it. For this reason he needs to repent from the deficiency of the repentance and doing that is due.

This again is not repentance, but repentance from not repenting. What is done is an obedience which does not require repentance. Only the missing part needs repentance. Repentance from repentance could be understood in one or two ways mentioned.

There is a third sense which is unique. That is a person who has achieved the level of intimacy with Allah in a way in which he finds devotion to Allah and engagement in remembering His bounties, His Names and Attributes most attractive, then he goes down from this condition to engage in repentance from a previous offence from which he had already repented, and is turned away from Allah. This is a shortcoming from which he is required to repent to Allah. This is the repentance from repentance because he descended from sincerity to breach.

The elegant and refined secret point of repentance is to look at the fault and failing to know Allah's will in that. He is the one who left you to commit it. Allah, the Most Glorious and Exalted, leaves a servant to fall in sin for two objectives:

One is to make him recognise His power, decision and kindness in covering it. In addition he has to realise that He gives respite for the one who commits an offence and is kind to accept his apology and to forgive him by His grace. The other is to confirm the evidence of His justice to him in order to punish him on committing a fault.

It is to be noted that when a man of discernment makes a mistake he has to look at five matters:
1. He should reflect on the command and prohibition of Allah, that will lead him to admit what he did was a mistake, and thus to confess his sin.

2. He has to ponder on threats and promises. That will create fear and awe which push him to repent.

3. He should also look at the fact that Allah enabled him and gave him power to commit it and decreed it for him. If He wanted, He would have saved him from it. This thought will produce varieties of knowledge of Allah, His Names, His Attributes, His wisdom, His mercy, His pardon and His forbearance and kindness. This knowledge will lead to learn the relation of the creation and command and threat and promise by His Names and Attributes. This vision will take him to beautiful meadows of knowledge and belief and the awareness of the secrets of the Decree and wisdom, which cannot be expressed in words. One of these secrets is that Allah the Almighty decrees what He wishes. He by His perfect power decrees for the servant and turns his heart and intention to the direction which He wishes. He makes him wish what He wants from him. The power of a man is restricted to act in his body and open areas. To make

him able to wish what He wants from him is only in the Hand of the Owner of great Might.

4. When a person recognises the power of his Lord and realises it by his heart, it will settle in his mind. His engagement in this realisation away from the humiliation of the fault is more beneficial to him because he now moves with Allah, not with his soul.

5. The knowledge of His might in His decrees will teach him that his affairs are decided by another being and he has no choice. He cannot get protection but by Him and no help is available to him except from Him. He is despicable and miserable in the hold of a Mighty Praiseworthy being.

Another aspect of the realisation of His power in His decree is to recognise that the perfection, praise, complete capability and might belong to Allah alone. The servant is to be blamed for failing, having fault, committing wrong and being in need. As his realisation of his shortcoming and need increases, his vision of Allah's power, perfectness and full ability will also grow.

Another feature is that a servant does not wish to disobey his Lord knowing that it is disobedience. When he comes to know that he is under the direction of another being and moves by his will and choice, his realisation of the power of Allah will grow. He will understand that he is free to choose while he is not, he has the right to wish but he is not and he has power to desire but he does not have. This will increase his realisation of Allah's might, greatness and perfect power.

Another good point for the person is to recognise the kindness of Allah Almighty, that He covered him at the time of committing the sin when He watched it. If He wanted, He would have exposed him to the people and humiliated him. Among the beautiful names of Allah is *al-Barr* (the Kind). This kindness to him emerges from His full perfectness and need of His servant to Him. He becomes occupied in the vision of this blessing and perception of this favour, grace and benefaction. In this situation he fails to remember his sin and remains with Allah Almighty. This is better for him than being occupied in his crime and remembering the disgrace of his sin. Being occupied with Allah and unmindful of other things is the most important objective and more brilliant aim. It does not mean to forget the sin altogether. If this situation occurs, he should turn to remembrance of his mistake and offence. For every time and condition there is devotion suitable to it.

Another feature is to recognise the clemency of Allah, in giving respite to the man who committed the sin. If He wished, He would have punished him promptly, but He is Clement and not in a hurry. This recognition will grant him an opportunity to perceive his Lord in His name of *al-Halim* (the Clement) and understand the attribute of His clemency. The benefit acquired through the sin is loved by Allah and is beneficial for the servant.

Another important aspect is the recognition of the servant of his Lord's magnanimity in accepting his excuse when he turns to Him, not by referring to decree. The Almighty accepts his excuse by virtue of His kindness and generosity. These encourage a man to engage in Allah's remembrance and gratitude. It produces another sort of love which was not available to him before that. It is because your love for the one, who thanks you on your good deeds and rewards you for them, then forgives your misdeeds and does not hold you accountable for them is far greater than your love for the good deeds alone. The devotion after the repentance is one thing and this is another.

Another point is to realise His grace in forgiving him. Forgiveness is a grace from Allah. Were He to hold you for His due, He would have been justified and still praiseworthy. But He forgave because of His grace, not because you deserved it. This act also makes you to give thanks to Him, to love Him and devote yourself to Him. You should express happiness and delight and recognise Him with His name *Al-Ghaffar* (the Most Forgiving). Acting in accordance to this quality is the most perfect love and knowledge.

Another point is that human states of humility, humbleness and servility to the Almighty lead to perfection. The soul has aspirations of similarity to the divinity and if given a chance it also could say atrocious things like Pharaoh (*"I am you Lord"*). The only way out of this type of thought is to surrender in humility to the Lord Almighty.

It has four stages:
1. The first stage is shared by all creatures, and that is the humility of need and poverty to Allah. The residents of the heavens and the earth are all in need of Him; He alone is free from need. All those who are in the heavens and the earth beg Him, but He does not ask anyone for anything.

2. The second stage is the submissiveness of obedience and devotion, which comes out of choice. It is for the people who are engaged in obeying Him, and this is the secret of servility.

3. The humbleness of love. A lover is humble by nature and in line to the degree of his love is his humbleness. Love is based on submissiveness to the beloved. It is said in a line of poetry: "Surrender and be humble to the one whom you love. In the case of love no nose is raised and contracted." Another poet said: "The people affected by love are poor. Even their graves are covered by the dust of humility among the graves."

4. The fourth stage is that of crime and sin.

When all these stages are combined, the humbleness and servility to Allah Almighty will be perfect and complete. In this case the believer surrenders to Allah with fear and awe, love and turning to Him, obedience and need and want. The essence of it is the poverty which is mentioned by the people of mysticism. It is in fact higher than to be called poverty. It is the core and secret of servility. To achieve this state is the most useful matter for the servant and the most beloved to Allah.

Another aspect is to understand that the beautiful Names of Allah require their results like causes require their effects. Allah's names 'All-Hearing, All-Seeing' require the object of hearing and seeing. In the same way His Names 'Most Forgiving, the Pardoning, the Relenting and the Clement' require someone who is to forgive, to pardon, to accept the repentance and to show clemency. They are the Attributes of perfection and as such they cannot exist without impact. This is what the most knowledgeable person i.e. the Prophet ﷺ, alluded to when he said, "If you do not commit sins, Allah will take you away and replace you with other people who will commit sins, then ask Him for forgiveness and He will forgive them."

If you imagine all living creatures extinct, then to whom will the Provider provide sustenance? If sins and disobedience disappear from the world, then who will the Most Forgiving forgive and pardon? Who will be turning to show His clemency and turn to accept his repentance? If the areas of needs are closed and all the people become free from need, then who will beg and implore? Who will the Almighty turn to show His favour, generosity and bounty?

Glory is to the One who made Himself known to His creatures with a variety of deeds and opened for them many paths, then indicated the right path and directed them to it: **"So that those who were to die might die after seeing a clear proof, and so that those who were to live might live after seeing a clear proof. Allah indeed is All-Hearing, All-Seeing."** *(8:42)*

Then there is the greatest secret which cannot be explained in words, but it is something which the hearts of the chosen people witness. It leads them to have more of the knowledge of their Lord and increase in yearning to Him and remembering Him much. It makes them able to realise the kindness, benevolence, and generosity of the Most Merciful. They come near to experience the secret of servility and essence of divinity. This is what is said in the Hadith reported by Anas ؓ that the Messenger of Allah ﷺ said, "Surely Allah is more pleased with the repentance of His servant, when he turns to Him in repentance, than if any one of you was travelling on your camel and the camel ran away from you, and it had your food and drink on it. Losing hope in finding it you came to a tree and lay down under its shadow. While you were in despair you notice your camel standing in front of you with all your provisions. You hold its noseband and say in utmost delight: 'My Lord, You are my servant and I am your Lord'. You made a mistake in your words because of the overwhelming joy".

This Hadith tells us that the words which slip from the mouth of a believer in the state of extreme joy or uncontrollable rage are not to be taken seriously. This servant is not going to be declared an unbeliever because of saying 'You are my servant and I am your Lord'. He spoke these words in ecstatic state.

A person has to know that Allah the Most High has chosen mankind from all other creatures through His favour, grace and honour. The Almighty created him for Himself and created everything for him. He singled out man for His love and knowledge and gave him privileges that He did not give to anything else. He put all that is in the heavens and the earth and between them under his control. He appointed the angels who are in a state of total obedience to Him to serve human beings. They protect him during his sleep and when he is awake and during his journeys and when he is at home. The Most Merciful sent His Books down to him and to chosen members of the community, and He sent to him His Messengers. He addressed them and spoke to them and chose from among them His friend and close companion. He made them the depository of His secrets and store of His wisdom. He created Paradise and Hell for them. The creation and command as well as the reward and punishment revolve around the human being. Human beings are the prime of the creations of Allah, and the aim of His commands and prohibitions, and for them is reward and punishment.

To put it briefly the human being has a status which no other being had been granted. Allah created their father by His hand, blew in him from His spirit and ordered His angels bow down to him and taught him the names of everything. He indicated his superiority over the angels and other creatures, and drove away the Devil from approaching him because he refused to bow down to him.

The believing man is the best of the creation and Allah's chosen person among the people. The Almighty created him, to shower His favours upon him and constantly confer His grace over him. He chose him to receive His bounty and honour in the way he never imagined. This favour cannot be achieved without the love of Allah, and His love can only be acquired by His obedience and putting His pleasure over everything else. If he fulfils his duties and carries out the orders of Allah, he will receive more favour and bounty, but if he fails in his duties then Allah will remove him from closeness.

There is an enemy for the man who is the most hateful creature to Allah. He is the Devil, who persuades His worshippers to devote themselves to him and worship him rather worship the true Being worthy of worship. He selected some people and composed from them his own party who obey him and follow his orders against their real Lord. Allah has clearly informed man about this enemy who is determined to deprive him of His favours. He warned him against his friendship and joining his party.

He, the Most Kind and Beneficent, told man that He is the most Generous of all, Most Honourable of all and the Most Merciful of all. His mercy overwhelms His wrath, His clemency overshadows His punishment and His forgiveness surpasses His censoring. He pours forth His grace over His creation and has taken it upon Himself to be merciful. He loves to be kind, generous, charitable and benevolent. All the bounty, good and favour are in His hand. The most beloved act for Him is to be kind to His servants, show mercy, cover them with His grace, and increase His support of them. He loves to make Himself known to them by His Names and Attributes and come close to them through His favours and benefaction.

Allah ﷻ is the Most Generous, and the generosity of everyone else who is created by Him or will be created is less than an atom compared to His Generosity. His desire to give and show kindness and favour is beyond the imagination of the people. His happiness for giving and supporting is greater than the happiness of the receiver who gets what he needs in the most difficult conditions. For Allah is the highest attribute. He feels happier when he gives than the person who gets when he is in dire need.

If the residents of the heavens and the earth, and the first and last of His creatures, the humans and Jinn, and the fresh and dry, stand together and ask Him and He gives everyone what they are asking for, it will still not reduce what He has by even an atom's weight.

He is Generous by Himself as He is Ever Living by Himself, All-Knowing, All-Seeing and All-Hearing by Himself. His great generosity is intrinsic to His being. Forgiving is dearer to Him than taking revenge. Mercy is more preferable to Him than punishing. Doing favours is more beloved to Him than dealing with justice, and giving is more favourable to Him than holding back.

In this condition when His servant and beloved, whom He created for Himself and granted him all kind of bounties, commits what causes His anger and turns away from Him to join His enemy and opens the door of punishment and revenge, he has indeed committed something which the Most Generous and Beneficent did not like for him. He proved by his offence that someone else is preferable to him than Allah and His favour.

It so happened that while this servant was busy in carrying out what His enemy wanted, all of sudden a thought struck his mind and he remembered his master's grace and favour and realised that he had to turn to Him. He knew that if he did not come to Him by his choice, he would be brought to Him in the worst condition. He then escaped from the town of His enemy to His safety. He hurried until he reached His door, and put his cheek on His doorstep. He laid his head there, imploring, begging, crying and expressing his regret. His master, knowing what was in his heart, showed mercy to him and was pleased with him. He replaced His punishment with pardon and His censor with clemency. By turning to Him in repentance he deserved from his Lord what is the prerequisite of His beautiful Names of Forgiving and Pardoning. How great will be the joy of his master with his act when His servant returned to Him by his choice and caused Him to open the door of kindness and benevolence which is dearer to Him than punishment and taking revenge.

Here it worth citing the famous story of a devoted person, who fled from his Lord. In the street, he noticed a boy crying and seeking help while his mother was chasing him until she drove him out of the house and closed the door. The boy walked a little distance then stopped and began thinking. He realised that there was no shelter for him other than the house from which he was banished, and no helper except his mother. He returned in grief and with a broken heart he found the door locked. He laid his head on the doorstep and went to sleep. His mother came out and when she saw him in that condition, she could not control herself and squeezed him to her lap, kissing him and crying. She asked him, "Where are you running to, away from me? Who else can give you refuge except me? Didn't I tell you not to disobey me and not to force me against my nature of mercy and affection to you? I always wanted good for you." Then she held him and they both entered the house.

The person who was watching contemplated the saying of the mother, "Don't force me by your disobedience against what I am created for to show mercy and affection." He then remembered the saying of the Messenger of Allah ﷺ, "Surely Allah is more affectionate to His servants than a mother is to her child."

However, when a servant causes his Lord to be angry with him, due to his sins, he has turned that mercy away from him. But when he turns to Him in repentance, he calls upon Him to do something which he deserves.

This is a small piece which will make you understand that Allah's happiness at seeing the repentance of His servant is greater than the joy of that person who lost his camel and then found it. This is the joy of Allah concerning His servants' repentance. But if you look at its connection with His being the object of worship, you will realise that it is far greater and more magnificent than this. This is something which can be realised only by the lovers of Allah.

Allah, the Glorious, created everything to worship Him, which means to love, show humbleness and obedience to Him. This is the truth for which the heavens and the earth have been created. He has not created them in vain. He has denied that He has not left human beings on their own. He, the Most High, loves to be worshipped and obeyed. He would not have cared about His creatures at all if they did not show their love for Him, obeyed Him and called upon Him.

When the servant opts out of performing the duty of obeying and worshipping Allah for which he was created, he has indeed deprived himself of the most beloved to Him. He got out of the purpose for which he was created, and became as though he was created in vain. His harvest did not produce the required fruit, but brought forth thorns and bushes. However if he returns to the objective for which he was created, then he has attained the most beloved goal to his Creator. He came out from the state of fruitlessness to the requisite of the wisdom of his creation. In this case the Lord's love of him will increase as He loves those who turn to Him in repentance and those who keep themselves clean.

Imagine if a person who you love was captured by your enemy and kept away from you, and you are aware that the enemy will subject him with terrible torment and all sorts of suffering. You have rights over him because you brought him up and trained him. Then he escapes from his captor and returns to you unexpectedly. You see him at your door, and he is seeking your help and trying to please you by every means, how will your happiness be? You brought him up for yourself and preferred him over anyone else.

You have to realise that you created him and did your favour to him. It is Allah, the Most Powerful, who created His devotee and amply bestowed His favour on him. He likes to bestow him with more bounties so that he becomes a manifestation of His graces. He wishes to see him giving thanks to His graces, expressing his love to the one who has given them to him and surrendering himself to Him in obedience and devotion. He would also like to see him hating and disobeying His enemy. Allah loves his devotee to treat His enemy as much as He likes to see him love his Creator and surrender to Him. This phenomenon will increase the love of Allah Almighty to His devotee and make Him happy.

It explains the happiness of Allah when His devotee fulfils the utmost requirement of his service. He, the Glorious, laughs to show His joy and happiness as He laughs when His devotee jumps from his bed to devote himself to the worship of Allah, reciting His verses. He also laughs at a man who was left alone in combat of his enemy and sold his soul to Allah and was killed for His love and pleasure.

He is happy with a man who keeps his charity secret and gives a beggar who was rejected by other people. This man secretly meets the beggar and gives to him without being noticed by anyone except Allah. There is nothing wrong in establishing these attributes to Allah. It is 'happiness' unlike any other, and laughing unlike any other.

PERSONAL EVALUATION OF SIN

A believer is required to look at the origin of the crime. It is the soul which enjoins evil. To look at it will bring him a number of benefits:

He learns that this soul is ignorant and unjust, and ignorance and injustice are the source of every bad action and statement. There is no hope in the reform of a person who is ignorant and unjust. A great deal of effort is to be made to give him useful knowledge which will get him out his ignorance. To put him away from injustice he needs to do plenty of good deeds. Such a person is in need of beseeching his Creator and Maker to protect him from the evil of his wicked soul and to purify it. Allah is the best to purify his soul, as He is the servant's Lord and Patron. He should pray to Allah not to surrender him to it, not for one moment, because if He did he would perish. No man has perished unless he was left to his soul. The Prophet ﷺ taught Husayn ibn al-Mundhr to say, "O Allah, inspire me to my good sense and save me from the evil of my soul."

The sermon of need taught by the Messenger of Allah ﷺ goes as follows:
"Praise is to Allah. We praise Him, seek help from Him, entreat Him for guidance and ask Him for forgiveness. We take refuge in Him from the evils of our souls and from our evil deeds."

Allah, the Most High, says:
"Those who are saved from the meanness of their souls are prosperous ones." *(64:16)*

The Almighty also said:
"The soul incites to evil." *(12:53)*

Anyone who knows the real essence and nature of his soul will realise that it is the source of every evil and abode of every misdeed. If a soul has any good in it, that is the bounty which Allah has favoured to it. Allah, the Most Glorious, has confirmed this in the following verse:
"If it were not for Allah's bounty and mercy towards you, not one of you would ever have attained purity." *(24:21)*

He also said:
"Allah has endeared faith to you and made it beautiful to your hearts; He made disbelief, mischief and disobedience hateful to you. It is people like this who are rightly guided." *(49:7)*

This love and hatred were not in the soul or by it, but it was Allah who favoured by them and for that the servant became amongst the rightly guided people.

"This was bounty and favour from Allah, and Allah is All-Knowing, All-Wise." *(49:8)*

He is well aware of those who are suitable for this bounty and who will be able to purify themselves by it, and He is wise enough that He does not place this bounty with those who do not deserve it and will ruin it.

REFLECTION ON SERVITUDE AND LORDSHIP
Here is another useful point to consider - anyone who knows himself and recognises the

rights of Allah, and is true in his quest, his reflection on his bad deeds will not leave a good deed for him. He will meet Allah in pure destitution and full poverty. This is because if he searches for the faults of his soul and shortcoming of his deeds, he will realise that they are not suitable for Allah. This commodity is not enough to acquire safety from the punishment of Allah, let alone to bring him great reward from Him. If he has sincere deeds and finds time to dedicate himself to Allah, he will comprehend the favour of Allah to him and understand that it is not from him but it is a favour from Allah, otherwise he did not deserve it. He is engaged constantly in observation of Allah's favour to him and the faults of his soul and deeds. Any time he contemplates he will be able to see it.

This is the most useful knowledge for the devotee, and for this reason the master of seeking forgiveness was the following supplication :
"O Allah, You are my Lord. There is no deity except You. You created me, and I am Your worshipper, and remain with my covenant and promise to You. I seek refuge in You from the evil of what I have done. I admit Your grace for me, and admit my sin, so forgive me. No one can forgive sins except You."

This supplication includes acknowledgement from the servant of Allah, Him being the object of worship. It also includes the recognition that He is the Creator of the world, and that He knows him. He brought him forth in a way that requires his inability to fulfil his duty. It also contains the admission of him being His servant whose forelock is in His hand and under His command. He cannot escape from Him, no one can help him beside Allah. He also confesses that he is bound by the command and prohibition which He passed to him on the tongue of His Messenger. He declares that he will do according to his capability, not in accordance to what is due to Him, because that is out of the power of humans. After confirming his belief in Allah's pledge and promise, the servant seeks His protection and support against the evil of the shortcoming in fulfilling His command and prohibition. He says, "If You do not give me refuge from the evil of my faults, I will perish. I confess my sins and take shelter in Your favour. From You comes favour and grace, and from me comes sins and mistakes. I beg You to forgive my sins, eradicate them and save me from their evil consequences. There is none but You who can forgive my sins."

This supplication was declared to be the master of seeking for forgiveness because it involves complete devotion. In this supplication, the servant admits the faults of his soul and his deeds and recognises the favours of Allah towards him.

Another area of contemplation is to look at the cause of the sin and the person who prompted him to commit it, and that is Satan. When the servant understands Satan's tricks, he considers him an enemy and tries his best to keep away from him and is vigilant against what he is after. The outcast Satan wishes to trap the believer in one of seven hurdles and stumbling blocks, some being more difficult than others. He does not abandon even the most difficult block unless his aim misses his target.

1. The first hurdle put in the person's way is to turn him from faith to disbelief in Allah and denial of His religion, meeting with Him and His perfect Attributes as His messengers have informed. If the Devil succeeds in his attempt at this point, the fire of his enmity cools off and he relaxes. But if his arrow passes through this hurdle by the guidance and light of faith, he tries to trap him in the second hurdle.

2. This is the hurdle of innovation. He puts in the person's mind notions against the truth, which Allah sent to His messengers with and revealed in His books. The Devil tries to make the man devote himself to Allah through acts and rituals which are actually invented and are unacceptable to the Almighty. The two acts of belief and action are attached to each other, rarely are separated. It is said by some scholars that innovation of belief is married to the innovation of acts, and that the marriage was consummated. This resulted in illegitimate children, who spread corruption amongst the Muslim Communities, causing the believers to complain to Allah Almighty. Satan fails in this stage when the believer crosses it with the light of the Sunnah and sticks to the way of the pious ancestors from the Companions and their followers. These type of people are very rare in the later periods. If someone remains on the right path, the people of innovations create problems for him and label him as 'innovator and misguided'.

3. When a devotee crosses the previous hurdle successfully, Satan then tries to deceive him by making him commit grave sins. He presents them in favourable shapes and opens the door of hope saying that faith revolves around belief and the acts are not important. He may put such words on his tongue which could lead to his destruction. For instance he may inspire him to say that "no sin is harmful with Tawhid as no good deed is useful with shirk."

Satan loves to be successful with the man at the point of innovation. It is because innovation demolishes religion and repels the message of the Messenger. The person involved in innovation does not shun it and repent from it, rather he invites others to it. He does not realise that it is the rejection of the Sunnah and attempt to put out the light of Allah. He embarks on turning things upside down and misguiding people and changing religion totally.

4. If the target of Satan escapes his tricks at this stage and crosses it successfully, Satan then attempts to involve him in minor sins. He puts in his mind that *if you avoid the major sins no harm will come to you if you commit some minor sins. Don't you know that keeping away from the major sins and by doing good deeds the minor sins are wiped out?* He persists on persuading him till the man commits the minor sins and continues doing them. This person is worse than someone who commits major sins and is scared and feels regret for it. To insist on the sin is

worse than the sin itself. No major sin remains with repentance and seeking forgiveness as no minor one remains minor with insistence.

The Messenger of Allah, blessing and peace of Allah be upon him, said, "Beware of little sins."

He gave an example of some people who stopped in a desert and found no wood for cooking. One of them then brought a piece of wood and another brought another until they collected enough firewood, lit the fire and cooked their food. The little sins pile on a man while he does not pay attention to them and they destroy him.

5. If the target of Satan gets away from his tricks by taking care and engaging in repentance and seeking forgiveness, he tries to deceive him through permissible matters. He keeps him busy with them and hinders him from doing more good deeds and preparing himself for the Hereafter. He tries to drag him to abandon the Sunnah acts and from it to abandon the obligatory acts. The least he gets from him that he causes him to lose great profits and a higher rank.

6. If the person gets away from this hurdle by full perception and complete light, and stays involved in carrying out good deeds and raising his status with Allah Almighty, the Devil tries to trap him in engaging in less important deeds. His enemy persuades him to get involved in them at the expenses of what is better and more valuable for him. He keeps him engaged with what is less than what is more, and with what is more beloved to Allah than what is only acceptable. There are very few people who reach this stage in the struggle with Satan. Most other people were taken up by him in the previous hurdles.

7. If the believer escapes from the tricks of the Devil at this stage because he understood the degrees of the deeds and their ranks with Allah, then he tries the last of his tricks. This hurdle is crossed only by the people of perfect knowledge and true perception who adopt the path of guidance and recognise the status of the deeds. This stage is very difficult and nobody can be saved from it. If anyone was to be saved, it would have been the messengers and prophets of Allah, who are the noblest people to Him. This stage involves Satan giving power to his soldiers to cause all sorts of troubles by hand, tongue and heart, in accordance to his rank in piety. As his rank goes higher, the enemy musters his cavalry and infantry against him. He gathers his forces against him and exerts his party and followers on him. It is not possible to escape this hurdle. As the believer strives earnestly to remain on the right path and carry out Allah's commands, the enemy strives to incite the foolish people against him. The devotee in this stage has put on the armour of the war and starts fighting the enemy of Allah for His sake and with His support. His devotion is that of the special worshippers and is known as the devotion of coercion, which is realised by the people of perfect understanding. Nothing is dearer to Allah than His enemy's irritation by His servant. Allah, the Most Glorious, has indicated this in

many places of His Book. He said:
"Anyone who migrates for Allah's cause will find many places of refuge (despite his enemy) and great resource in the earth." *(4:100)*

The Almighty also said:
"That is because if they are afflicted with any thirst, weariness, or hunger in Allah's cause, take any step that angers the disbelievers, or gain any advantage over an enemy, a good deed is recorded in their favour on account of it. Allah does not waste the reward of those who do good." *(9:120)*

Allah Almighty illustrated the condition of the Messenger of Allah ﷺ and the believers in the following words:
"Their description in the Gospel is as a plant which produces its offshoot, strengthens it, and it grows firm to stand upon its stalk, delighting the owners, so that He may infuriate the disbelievers by it." *(48:29)*

It shows that irritation of the disbelievers is a desired goal of the Lord. To achieve it is the perfect devotion.

Whoever devotes himself to Allah by infuriating His enemy, he has acquired full share of being true servant. He will get his reward in line with the love of the servant for his Lord and friendship or enmity of His enemy. For this reason strutting between the lines against the enemy is praised. To feel happy after giving charity secretly, which is not known to anyone except Allah, is also appreciated because Satan does not like it. This is a part of devotion which is known only to few people. The one who tastes its delight, weeps over his past days.

With Allah is the support as on Him is the trust, and there is no power and no strength except with Allah. These are a few unique secrets of repentance. Do not mock them. You may not find them in any other book. From Allah is the favour and bounty, and from Him comes the help.

Many people do not distinguish between the love and pleasure of Allah and His will and decree. They are mainly *Jabariyyah* and *Qadariyyah*. They claimed that the will and love are the same or inseparable. Many of them believe that since He willed, all acts are loved by the Lord. The result of this belief was that they do not consider any evil as evil and any abominable act as disliked.

The *Qadariyyah* claimed that since the sins are not accepted by Him, they are out of His will and creation. The Qur'an and the Sunnah, the reason, natural instinct and the consensus declare that the will and love are two different matters. Allah, the Most High, said about the hypocrites:

"They try to hide themselves from people, but they cannot hide from Allah. He is with them when they plot at night, saying things that do not please Him." *(4:108)*

The Almighty declared that He does not accept what they plot in the night, including false accusation, charging an innocent, giving false witness and acquitting the criminal. All the Muslims agree that what Allah wills, takes place and what He does not want does not happen. No group disagreed with this except the *Qadariyyah* who say that He wills what does not take place and what He does not will takes place.

The view of the early scholars and leaders is that although the evils take place with His will and decree, they are hateful to Him. He is the Creator of what He loves and that which He dislikes. Just like the substances which are created by Him while among them are those whom He hates and loathes like the Devil and his party and other wicked species. There are on the other hand those whom He likes and loves like His prophets, messengers, angels and His friends. In the same way all the actions are created by Him. Among them are desirable and undesirable ones. He has created undesirable matters for His wisdom. He said: **"Allah does not like corruption,"** *(2:205)* though it is found by His will and decree.

He also said:
"If you are ungrateful, remember Allah has no need of you, and He is not pleased by ingratitude in His servants. If you are grateful, He is pleased with it for you." *(39:7)*

Ingratitude and gratefulness take place with His will and decree, but one of them is loved by Him and the other is hateful to Him.

Allah, the Glorious, commanded us to keep away from shirk, injustice, the abominable acts and arrogance, then He said:
"The evil of all these actions is hateful to your Lord." *(17:38)*

These actions are distasteful to Him, though they take place with His will and decree. In an authentic report the Messenger of Allah ﷺ said, "Allah dislikes three things for you: idle talk, asking too many questions and wasting of money."

This disliking is for things which are found with His will. In another Hadith reported in Musnad of Imam Ahmad the Prophet ﷺ said, "Allah likes His concessions to be taken up as He dislikes His prohibited matters to be committed."

This statement contains liking and disliking for two things which existed by His will. There are many examples in the Qur'an and the Sunnah.

Allah Almighty has put in the minds of His servants to say: 'Allah loves this act, and He dislikes that act and so and so does what Allah does not like.'

There are many statements in the Qur'an regarding the displeasure and wrath of Allah on His enemies. Displeasure of Allah is the cause of torment and curse. He said:

"If anyone kills a believer deliberately, the punishment for him is Hell, and there he will remain forever. Allah is angry with him and curses him and has prepared a tremendous torment for him." *(4:93)*

The Almighty in this verse has separated His torment, anger and curse, and made each one different from the other. The Prophet ﷺ used to pray, "O Allah, I seek refuge in Your pleasure from Your anger; I seek refuge in Your forgiving from Your punishment and seek refuge in You from You."

Consider the Prophet's seeking refuge in the quality of pleasure from the quality of anger, and in the quality of forgiveness from that of punishment. He has attached both to Allah and declared that each of them belong to Him and no one else. He says that *what I am seeking protection from takes place with Your will and decree, and the pleasure and forgiveness in which I seek refuge are also by Your will and decree. If You wish to be pleased with and forgive Your servant it is up to You, and if You decide to be angry and punish him it is up to You. My protection from what I dislike and fear is by Your will. All the good and bad matters are by Your decree and will. I seek refuge in Your power, strength, might, mercy and benevolence from what may take place by Your power and might, justice and wisdom. I am seeking refuge in no one but You from anything which takes place by Your will and decree. You are the one who are able to give me protection by Your will from that which takes place by Your will.*

The sense of Tawhid, knowledge and devotion hidden in these words can be perceived only by those who are well informed of Allah, know Him perfectly and understand the meaning of devotion to Him.

We have briefly described some of their sense. If we tried to give a full explanation, it would require a very large book. However, the door has been opened for you. If you enter, you will see what no eye has seen, no ear has heard of and no mind has imagined.

The division of matters to be liked and disliked by Allah is recognised by reason and texts. Those who deny it are going against what Allah has created His servants for, and is going against the logic and scripture.

Allah, the Most Powerful, designated for some reason grave punishments in the world and the Hereafter for the sinners. This was because His anger for those who do wrong acts became so great that He decided to cause them a variety of calamities. On the other hand, His love of the good deeds which He likes made Him love those who do them, and show His favour to them. They are His friends. The origin of befriending is love as the root cause of enmity is dislike or hate.

SUMMARY OF RULES ABOUT REPENTANCE

Here are some important rules, the knowledge of which is certainly needed and no one should ignore them. They are as follows:

1. To turn to Allah in repentance immediately after committing a sin without any delay is obligatory. To delay it is disobedience. When a person repents in this case, he has to repent again for delaying his turning to Allah. This is something which a person rarely thinks of.

2. He believes that when he turned to Allah in repentance, he has fulfilled his duty and there is nothing else for him to do. He is not aware that a second penitence is required for delaying his repentance.

3. Only a general repentance from all sins, what he is aware of and what he is unaware of, can rescue him. In fact what a person is not aware of from his sins is more than what he knows. His unawareness of them is of no use to him if he has an opportunity to learn about them. In this case he has committed the offence of abandoning the knowledge and act together. His crime is more serious. The Messenger of Allah ﷺ said, "Association with Allah (shirk) in this community is more hidden than the crawling of an ant."

4. Abu Bakr ؓ asked: 'How can we get rid of it, Messenger of Allah?' He replied, "By saying: 'O Allah, I seek refuge in You from associating partner to You while I am aware; and seek forgiveness from what I am not aware."

5. It is to seek forgiveness of Allah from the sins He knows and the servant does not know.

6. It is said in an authentic report that the Prophet ﷺ used to pray in his prayer, "O Allah, forgive me my mistakes and my ignorance, my excess in my affairs and what You are more aware than me. O Allah, forgive me my serious and jestful acts, mistaken and deliberate deeds, and all these are with me. O Allah, forgive me what I have done earlier and later, what I have done secretly and openly and what You are more aware than me. You are my Lord, there is no god except You."

In another Hadith he is reported to have said, "O Allah, forgive me all my sins, small and big mistakes and deliberate, secret and open, the first and the last."

This general and comprehensive prayer is to include repentance from what the servant is aware of and what he is not.

REPENTANCE FROM A SIN WHILE INSISTING ON ANOTHER

Is the repentance from a sin while insisting on another is correct? There are two opinions of the learned scholars in this regard.

It is a serious and difficult question. Nothing certainly can be said without convincing evidence. There are those who claim that it is a correct argument that when a person embraces Islam, which means repentance from disbelief, while retaining some sinful acts before Islam, which he did not repent, all are forgiven. In the same way when he repents from one sin while committing another, it will be judged accordingly depending on his intention.

Others have refuted this claim by saying that Islam is different and it has a status which nothing else has. It has power and an effective role to include a child by the faith of his parents or one of them. Also a slave child is considered to be Muslim if his captor and owner is Muslim. It is due to the power of Islam and the interest of the religion that it is effective even in the case of subordination without intention.

They also argued that repentance means to return to Allah and to His obedience after disobeying Him. How can a person who repents from one sin yet consistently commits thousands of other offences be considered to return to Allah?

They further said that Allah does not censure a person who repents sincerely because he has returned to the servitude and obedience of Allah. But a man who persistently gets involved in sins has not returned to the obedience of the Lord and has not repented sincerely.

They also said that when a person who turns to Allah in repentance is no more disobedient than when an unbeliever embraces Islam, he is no more called an unbeliever. However, if a person after repenting from one sin persistently commits another, he is considered disobedient and as such his repentance is not correct.

The core of the problem is whether repentance can be divided into portions like the sin, so a man can be considered repenting from one aspect, excluding the other aspect as is the case with Islam and belief?

The preferable view is that it is subject to division. It differs in its quality as it differs in its quantity. If a servant performs an obligatory duty and abandons another, he deserves punishment on what he has abandoned, not on what he has done. The same applies to the case of a man who repents from one sin and commits another. Repentance is required from both sins, but he fulfilled his duty regarding one case and abandoned the other. What he neglected will not be the cause of destroying what he has done. It is similar to the case of a man who neglected the pilgrimage and fulfilled the duty of performing prayer, paying zakat and fasting.

The opponents of the above view say that repentance is one act which means to refrain from what Allah does not approve, to regret and to turn to His obedience. If it is not found with all its parts, it is not correct. It is one act of worship. To carry out one part yet leave out another is like performing part of the act of worship and abandoning the other. The parts of an act of worship are connected with one another more firmly than the connection of various acts of worship with one another.

The holders of the other view say that every sin has repentance peculiar to it. It is a duty on the man and has no connection with other repentance exactly as a sin has no connection with another.

My view in this question is that repentance from one sin while persistently committing another of its kind is not valid. Repentance from one sin while committing another different one which is not of the same kind or related to it is correct and valid. For instance, if a man repents from usury but did not abandon drinking wine, his repentance from usury is correct. But if he repents from *Riba al-fadl* (usury of unequal exchange) and did not repent from *Riba al-nasi'ah* (the usury of delay in payment) or vice versa and persistently is involved in it, his repentance is not valid. The same applies to a man who repents from smoking hashish but insists on drinking wine or vice versa, and the man who repents from committing adultery with a woman and continues doing it with another. These people in reality have not repented; they moved from one kind to another. It is different to the case of a person who moved from a sin to another different one. He may have different reasons for this change. They may be that the second sin is lighter or the motive for it is so strong that he is unable to control himself or it is easily available to him, or his friends and associates overwhelm him and do not give him a chance to repent, and he enjoys good status among them and does not want to lose it. If a man from this kind of people repents from killing or taking illegally the wealth of innocents or consuming money belonging to orphans, but did not repent from drinking wine or committing adultery, his repentance from the offences he has committed is right and he is not going to be accountable for that. He will have to answer the crimes he is persistently involved in. Allah knows best.

ADDITIONAL RULES RELATED TO REPENTANCE
Is it a condition for repentance to be right, that the man should never commit a sin, or it is not a condition?

Some people impose this condition and say that once he repeated the sin it becomes clear that his repentance was not right, but invalid. However, the majority of scholars are of the opinion that it is not a condition. The validity of repentance depends on refraining from the sin, regretting it and having a firm intention of not committing it again. If the offence concerns a human being then is it necessary for him to redress it? There is more elaboration about it which will be discussed soon. If a person repeats the offence when he has made a firm resolution to not repeat it, he will be considered as committing the sin for the first time and his previous repentance is not affected.

The issue is based on a rule. That is when a man repented from a crime then committed it again will the sin of the previous crime return to him and he will deserve the punishment for both the previous and the current one if he dies in his persistence? Or will his previous sin be wiped out, and he will only be punished for this later one?

There are two opinions concerning this. Some people say that the sin of the first crime will return because his repentance was invalid because he repeated the offence. They argue that repentance is like turning from disbelief to Islam. When a disbeliever embraces Islam all his sins of disbelief and other offences are wiped out. But if he reverts back, his earlier sins will return with the sin of apostasy. The Messenger of Allah ﷺ said, "Whoever does good deeds in Islam will not be asked about his deeds before becoming Muslim. On the other hand if anyone commits bad deeds after accepting Islam, he will be responsible for the previous and the current misdeeds."

This is the situation of a man who accepted Islam but committed offences, and apostasy is the greatest offence. Such a person's Islam which is surrounded from both sides with sins will not avail him. In the same way the repentance that came between two offences will not obliterate the previous sin, and the man will be responsible for it together with the current one.

They also said that the validity of the repentance was attached with the condition of fulfilling its requirements, and something which is attached with a condition becomes null and void when the condition disappears. It is the same with Islam. It is valid only when its requirements are fulfilled.

They further said that repentance is obligatory throughout life. Its requirements must be followed at every stage of life. It is like abstaining from what breaks the fast of the day. If a person abstains most of the day and gets involved in matters that spoil his fast, his fast of that day is destroyed and he becomes like the one who did not abstain at all.

They referred to the saying of the Messenger ﷺ: "A man does the deeds of the people of Paradise until there remains between him and Paradise no more than an arm's length, and the written Decree comes into effect and he does the deed of the people of Hell and enters it."

This statement includes all the acts, whether the last offence is disbelief which will cause eternal punishment or a sin which will lead the person to Hellfire. The Prophet did not say that "the man renounces Islam." He only said that he does an act which leads him to Hell. In a version in some Sunan collections the Prophet is reported to have said, "A man engages in the deeds of obedience of Allah for sixty years, but when his death approaches, he commits injustice in his will and goes to Hell."

It is clear that the last bad act includes disbelief or sinful acts. The crucial factor is what is done at the end. Someone may raise a question here that your statement implies that good deeds are destroyed by bad deeds. This is the view of the *Mu'tazilah*. But the Qur'an and the Sunnah declare that the good deeds destroy the bad one and not the other way round. Allah said: **"Good deeds do away with misdeeds."** *(11:114)*

The Prophet ﷺ said to Mu'adh ؓ, "Be mindful of Allah wherever you are and follow an evil act with a good one, to wipe out the evil one. Treat people with noble character."

The answer is that both the Qur'an and the Sunnah indicate distinctly unequal positions of good and bad deeds. The Qur'an cannot be rejected because of the view of the *Mu'tazilah*. Rather we accept the truth from anyone and reject the falsehood from any source. The distinctly unequal positions of good and bad deeds are cited in many places in the Qur'an, for instance 7:8-9; 21:47; 23:101-111; 101; and 69: 19-37.

As for the destruction of good deeds by evil acts, Allah the Most High, said: **"You who believe, obey Allah and His Messenger: do not invalidate your deeds."** *(47:33)*

Invalidation here has been explained as renouncing Islam. It is the greatest cause of invalidation of deeds though it is not the only cause. Allah also said: **"You who believe, do not invalidate your charities by reminders and hurtful words."** *(2:264)*

Here two causes i.e. reminder and hurting happened after the charities and destroyed them. Almighty compared their invalidation by reminder and hurting with the charity of a person who gives to show off: both charities are invalidated. Allah, the Exalted, also said: **"You who believe, do not raise your voices above the voice of the Prophet or be loud to him in speech like the loudness of some of you to others, lest your deeds become worthless while you do not perceive."** *(49:2)*

These are some examples from the Qur'an. In the Hadith the Messenger of Allah ﷺ said, "Whoever, misses deliberately the 'Asr prayer his deeds are destroyed."

'A'ishah ﷺ said to the slave girl of Zayd b. Arqam who had sold on the basis of sample, "Tell Zayd that his jihad with the Messenger of Allah, peace be on him, has been wasted unless he repents".

Imam Ahmad stated that it is better for a man who is afraid of committing adultery to get married by taking a loan so that he does not commit illegal acts and waste his good deeds.

When it is established that there are evil deeds which destroy the good ones, it is possible that repeating an evil act destroys the good result of repentance. In such a case, repentance becomes as though it did not take place, and both evil deeds - the previous and the current - will come together.

Since the Qur'an and the Sunnah and the consensus of the scholars establish the equal weight of the good and bad deeds, the more superior one of them will be effective. Ibn Mas'ud said, "The people will be judged on the Day of Resurrection and anyone whose evil deeds are more than his good deeds by one item, he will end in Hell. On the other hand whoever's good deeds are more by one matter, he will go to Paradise". Then he recited from the Qur'an:
"Those whose deeds are heavy on the scale will be the successful. And those whose good deeds are light- they are the ones who will lose themselves for what they were doing towards Our verses." *(7:8-9)*

He added: "The scale becomes heavy or light by one small unit". Then he went on: "Those, whose good and evil deeds are equal they will be placed on *Al-A'raf* (the heights)".

"Good deeds wipe out the evil ones" *(11:114)*

The question here is that if the good deeds are superior to the evil ones by one unit, will they cancel all evil deeds and will the person will be rewarded for all good deeds or the good deeds matching the evil will be cancelled and he will not get reward for them? In the same way if the evil deeds are more by only one unit, will the person go to Hell by that one deed which was in surplus or by all? There are two views of the people who hold the opinion of equal weight.

The other group believes that the responsibility of the sin from which a person repented does not return to him after violating the repentance and committing the sin again. They say that the sin has been wiped out by his repentance and become as though he did not commit it. He will be responsible for the new offence and not for the previous one.

They claim that it is not a condition for the validity of the repentance that the person should not commit a sin throughout his life. When he regrets and resolves to keep away from that sin, its responsibility is removed from him. When he resumes, the responsibility comes back. It is not like disbelief, which destroys good deeds. Disbelief is a different matter and therefore it destroys all good deeds. To commit a sin again does not destroy good deeds done before it.

They further argued that repentance is one of the greatest deeds. If it were to be destroyed by committing the sin again, it will destroy all other good deeds. It is certainly false, and resembles the view of the *Khawarij*, who declare a man who commits a grave sin as an unbeliever. It is also like the view of the *Mu'tazilah*, who condemn a man to Hell forever for committing a grave sin, even though he may have done thousands of good deeds. Both sects agree on the eternal punishment of the person who commits a grave sin. The difference between the two is that the *Khawarij* declare such person as disbeliever and the *Mu'tazila* considers him as disobedient. Their views are invalid in Islam and against the text and logic and the requirement of the justice. Allah declared in the Qur'an:

"Surely Allah does not do wrong to anyone even as much as an atom's weight; while if there is a good deed, He multiplies it and gives a great reward from His own." *(4:40)*

Imam Ahmad recorded in his Musand that the Prophet ﷺ said, "Allah loves a servant who is tempted (to commit a sin) and repents."

I say that this is a man who whenever tempted by a sin, repents from it. If committing the sin again was to destroy his repentance, he would not have been loved by the Lord; rather he would have been the subject of His wrath. Allah, the Most Glorious, attached the validity of repentance with seeking forgiveness and avoiding the persistence. He did not mention repeating the sin. He said:

"Those who, when they commit an immoral act or wrong themselves, remember Allah and seek forgiveness for their sins – and who can forgive sins except Allah? And they do not persist in what they have done while they know." *(3:135)*

Persistence means to decide to commit a sin whenever it is possible. This is what prevents the repentance of a person to be granted.

They further argued that abiding by the requirements of repentance is a condition for the perfection and usefulness of repentance. It is not a condition for the validity of it. The acts of worship such as fasting and prayer are different. They are one act and will not be valid unless all requirements are carried out. Repentance on the other hand is various acts related to various sins. Each sin has its own repentance. If someone does one act and abandons another, what he abandoned is not going to affect what he did. It is like a man who fasts a day of Ramadan and breaks it without any excuse. Will his breaking fast of that day annul the reward of the days he fasted? Or if a man performs prayer but does not fast, or he paid zakat but did not perform Hajj, will what he did not do spoil the reward of those acts which he did?

CHAPTER FOUR
DILEMMA OF SINNING VS REPENTANCE

EVIL DEEDS DO NOT SPOIL THE GOOD ONES

The point is that previous repentance is a good deed, and committing the sin again is an evil deed. This act is not going to spoil the good deed as it will not spoil other good deeds done at the same time. This is clear according to the views of the followers of the Sunnah. They agree that a man may be loyal to Allah and disloyal to Him at the same time, from two different perspectives. He may be loved by Allah and hated by Him from two different angles. A man may harbour belief and hypocrisy and belief and disbelief at the same time. Allah said:

"On that day they were closer to disbelief than belief." *(3:167)*

"Most of them do not believe in Allah except while they associate others with Him." *(12:106)*

The Almighty confirmed their faith in Him with association of others. If they deny the messengers with association of others with Allah, their faith will not avail them at all. On the other hand if they accept the messengers and in the meantime commits acts of shirk, they are not excluded from the believers in Messengers and the Hereafter. They deserve the threat more than the people who commit grave sins.

Their association (shirk) is of two kinds, hidden and open. The hidden one may be forgiven, but Allah will not forgive the open one without repentance, as Allah does not forgive association of partners with Him. Following this principle the followers of the Sunnah hold that the people who commit grave sins will go to Hell, and then will be taken out from it and sent to Paradise.

When it is established, then it becomes clear that the man who committed the sin again is hated by Allah from one aspect and is loved by Him because of his repentance and earlier good deeds. Allah will make each cause effective in his case with wisdom and justice and will not do injustice even an atom's weight.

"Your Lord is not unjust to the servants." *(41:46)*

If his new evil deeds overwhelm his old good deeds and cancel them, and then he makes sincere repentance, his previous good deeds will return to him. It will not be like resuming his deeds. He will be told: 'You repented for the good deeds you sent forward. The good deeds you did during your Islam are greater than what a disbeliever does, like freeing a slave, giving out charity and being kind to relatives, all in the condition of disbelief. Hakim b. Hizam said to the Messenger of Allah ﷺ: 'Messenger of Allah, tell me about what I did before being Muslim, such as freeing slaves, the charity I gave and kindness which I showed to my relatives - am I going to get any reward for that? The Prophet replied, "You became Muslim with all the good you sent forward".

This was because the evil deeds committed between the two good acts were removed by repentance and became as though they did not exist. Now the two acts of obedience joined together.

THE CASE OF A PERSON WHO WAS UNABLE TO COMMIT A SIN
Another question about repentance is that if a person was unable to commit a sin because something prevented him, is the repentance of this person correct? The example is a liar, whose intention was to accuse a chaste woman of fornication, and a man who gives false witness and has his tongue chopped off. Or an adulterer, whose organ is cut off, or a thief whose all four limbs were amputated and a counterfeiter whose hand was cut off or a person who reached a point where the motives of sins which he used to commit are no more available to him: what is the status of the repentance of these people?

There are two views regarding the issue:
Some people say that such people's repentance is not valid because repentance is to come from a person who is capable of carrying out the act or abandoning it. The repentance is from what is possible not from what is impossible. This is like repenting from moving a mountain from its place, drying out the seas, flying in the air and so on so forth. These are the acts which are beyond the capacity of a man.

They went on arguing that the repentance means to resist the motive of the soul and respond to the motive of the truth. Here there is no motive for the soul because it is clear that the act is impossible.

They further said that it was like someone who was forced to abandon the act and such people's repentance is not valid.

They continued that it is established in the reasons and nature of people that the repentance of insolvents and those affected by disasters is not considered and it is not correct. It is called the repentance of insolvency and disaster. It is also supported by many texts that confirm that the repentance when the thing is before one's eyes is not useful. It is the repentance of exigency and not of choice. Allah Almighty said:
"The repentance accepted by Allah is only for those who do evil out of ignorance and then repent soon after. It is those to whom Allah will turn in forgiveness, and Allah is Ever-Knowing, All- Wise. The repentance is not accepted of those people who continue to do evil until when death comes to one of them, he then says, 'Now I repent,' or of those who die while they are disbelievers. We have prepared a painful torment for them." *(4:17-18)*

Ignorance here means the ignorance of an action even if the man has knowledge. Qatada said, 'All the Companions of the Messenger, Allah's blessing and peace be on him, agree that any deed whether done deliberately or otherwise which includes disobedience of Allah is ignorance. Anyone who disobeys Allah is ignorant.'

As far as the phrase 'repent soon after' is concerned, it is explained by the majority of the commentators as repentance which is done before realising that death is near, or before witnessing the angel of death. It is also said that it means that the person repents while he is healthy before falling to his deathbed. Ibn Umar reported the Messenger of Allah ﷺ saying, "Allah accepts the repentance of the servant before he breathes his last."

It is also reported from the statements of the Prophet ﷺ that Satan said, "By Your might, my Lord, I will continue misguiding Your servants as long as their souls are in their bodies." Allah replied, "By My might and power I will continue forgiving them as long as they seek My forgiveness."

When a person repents at the time of death his repentance will not be accepted because he is doing is out of exigency and not by choice. It is like repenting after the sun rises from the west or on the Day of Resurrection or after witnessing the torment of Allah.

The advocates of the view that the repentance of a man who was unable to commit the crime is not accepted also argued that the essence of repentance is to hold the soul against the work which is forbidden. Abstaining is possible from a matter which is in the power of a man. Abstaining from what is impossible is unthinkable. Moreover, repentance means to abstain from the sin and in the case of this person it is impossible.

The second view - which is the correct one - is that the repentance of such a man is valid and possible. All the essential requirements of the repentance are found and he has regrets. It is said in a Hadith that "regret is repentance." If his regret is sincere and he blames himself then this is what repentance is. How can he be denied of repentance when he reproaches himself and regrets his acts? Especially when he is scared, distressed and cries and has a firm resolve that if he were healthy and capable of doing the thing, he would not do it. If the Lord can put a man who is incapable of doing some good deeds in the position of the one who has done it because of his sincere intention, how can He ignore the intention of this man? It is reported in an authentic Hadith that the Prophet ﷺ said, "When a servant falls sick or travels, the good deeds he was doing whilst he was healthy or resident are recorded for him."

The Prophet also said in an expedition, "There are people in Madinah who were with you each time you marched or crossed a valley. These are the people who were held back by some excuses at Madinah."

This is the case of those who were unable to join the Muslims in their expedition. In the same way those who were prevented from committing a sin because of incapability and had good intention should be treated like those who kept away from sin by their choice. It is clear that the harm of a sin for which there is a threat arises sometimes from the intention and sometimes from doing it. In the case of this incapable person there is no harm to be seen and the punishment follows the harm.

The difference between this person and the one who repents after witnessing the event happening on the Day of Resurrection is that once the promised time comes the responsibility is lifted. The repentance can be made only in the period of responsibility. This incapable person is still responsible and commands and prohibitions apply to him. To keep away from the evil is conceivable for him. He loved to do it and felt sad on missing it, but now he feels regret and grief on doing it.

A DILEMMA OF A MAN WHO CRAVES FOR A SIN ALTHOUGH HE INTENDS TO REPENT

Another case is that if a person had started committing a crime then he made the intention to repent, but it was not possible for him to do so unless he committed some of the sin, what would be the ruling concerning him? For example, if a man committed adultery and put his organ in the vulva of a strange woman and then the thought of repentance came to his mind before pulling out his organ. Or a person who walked in a land which was taken illegally then he intended to repent. Now both of them cannot come out without having committed the sin. How can they then repent from a prohibited matter by another prohibited one?

This is a difficult question. Some people have said that he was not responsible for the part of the sin he got involved in to get out of the crime. They said that the action cannot be commanded because it is forbidden but there is no way of getting out. So it could be said that in this part of crime he was not under responsibility.

Another group is of the view that the second part of his action is obligatory and unlawful. It has two dimensions - from one side he is under obligation and from the other he is prohibited. There are many other examples of a matter being obligatory and forbidden at the same time, such as performing prayer in a land taken illegally. Here the prayer is obligatory but to do it in that land is prohibited. Another example is covering the body with silk; covering the body is obligatory but wearing silk is unlawful.

The correct view is that pulling out the organ and getting out of the illegally taken land are repentance which is not prohibited. The person is commanded to repent and it is impossible that he is commanded doing the prohibited act. Pulling out of the organ, which is part of the intercourse, was forbidden if it was enjoyed and if the action was completed. But if the intention was to avoid a forbidden matter and to stop the enjoyment, then there is no evidence for it being prohibited.

It is inconceivable that these cases have no ruling from Allah. His ruling is to withhold illegal intercourse and get out of the land immediately. To dispose of the possession of another person is unlawful when causing harm is intended. But if the intention is to desist from enjoyment and to remove the harm from the owner then it is not forbidden by Allah and His Messenger and there is no logical evidence for it.

THE DUES OF THE HUMAN BEINGS MUST BE PAID
Another ruling of repentance is that if the crime involves the financial or physical right of a human, repentance requires that it must be restored to him or he be informed and forgiveness is sought from him. The Prophet 繠 said, "Whoever has done wrong to his brother concerning his wealth or honour should get it settled now before a day comes where there will be no dinar or dirham except the good or evil deeds."

Regarding slandering or accusation, the question is whether it is necessary as part of the repentance that the man admits his crime and tells the affected person that he had insulted him without mentioning the offence, or it is enough that he repents between himself and Allah without telling the man?

There are three views in this respect:
There are two statements from Ahmad concerning accusation of adultery, and whether it is necessary to inform the accused and ask him to pardon or not. The well known view of al-Shafi'i, Abu Hanifah and Malik as recorded in the books of their scholars is that the affected person must be informed.

Their argument is that the offence contains two rights, one of Allah and the other of the person concerned. The right of the man will be fulfilled by telling him and seeking pardon from him, and the right of Allah will be fulfilled by regretting the offence. They said that it is supported by the fact that the repentance of a murderer will not be complete unless he surrenders himself to the guardian of the diseased, who has the choice of taking retaliation or forgiving.

The other view that it is not necessary for the offender to tell the man concerned; it will be enough that he repents to Allah for his misdeed. He should speak about the person opposite of what he had said. So, he should praise him in the place he had slandered him, and speak of his modesty and chastity where he had accused him of committing adultery. In the meantime seek Allah's forgiveness for his victim. This is the view is chosen by Ibn Taymiyyah.

The scholars who hold this opinion say that telling the concerned person is pure scandalous and does not include any benefit. By knowing what was said the man will feel hurt and distressed while he was comfortable before that. After hearing what was said he may not be able to sustain it and may be affected psychologically or physically. This type of act is not allowed in the Shari'ah.

They further said that telling the man may lead to enmity between him and his accuser, producing permanent hatred and an evil greater than the evil of slandering and accusation. The religious teachings are to create sympathy, mutual understanding and good feeling.

There is a difference between the financial rights and personal offences. In the case of financial offence the man may be benefitted if his rights are returned to him, unlike the slandering and accusation which do not bring any good to him, but would rather cause him distress.

So, in the case of financial misdeeds the man knows he will be pleased, whereas telling the bad things which were said will only cause him unhappiness and distress throughout his life. There is a marked difference between two situations and it is wrong to compare one with the other.

DOES REPENTANCE ABSOLVE THE SIN?

Another question concerning repentance is if a servant repents from the sin will he go back to the status which he had before committing the sin or not? The matter is disputed. Some scholars say that he will go back to his former position because repentance wipes out the sin completely and makes it as though it never happened.

They further say that repentance is a great and virtuous deed. If his sin had dropped him from his status, his repentance would raise him back to it. Its likeness is as a man who fell in a well and had a compassionate friend who let down a rope, which the man held in order to come out of the well to reach the place where his friend was. The repentance and good deeds are like that compassionate friend and sympathetic brother.

Others say that the person would not go back to his former status because he was not in a static state but was rising up. When he committed the sin he started going down, and when he repented the degree of ascendance was reduced. Its likeness is as two people who were walking on the same path, then one of them went back or stopped for some reason while his colleague continued walking. When this person resumed his walk and followed his colleague, he was never able to reach him. Whilst he proceeded ahead, his colleague went further ahead. They say that the walking man walked with the power of his faith and deeds. When he walked fast, his power increased, and the man who halted, his power of faith was weakened and his pace was slowed.

I heard Shaykh al-Islam Ibn Taymiyyah saying, "The correct view is that there are those who will not return to their status after repentance and others who will return to their former position. Yet there are those who will gain a higher position than the previous one and become better than they were before committing the sin. Dawud became better after repentance than he was before committing the offence. This depends on the condition of the man after repentance and his earnestness, resolve, caution and seriousness. If these qualities are higher than they were before the sin, he will gain a higher rank than before. He will return to the similar status if they are the same and if they are lower than before, he will go lower as well." The Shaykh's statement clears the position.

This could be illustrated by two examples:
The first is of a man who is proceeding on his way with peace and tranquility. He runs once and walks again, and takes rest and sleeps another time. While he was on his journey, he saw a beautiful shadow, cold water, a place of rest and a shining meadow. He wanted to stop and rest there. Before he reached this place, an enemy jumped on him, arrested him, shackled him and prevented him from walking. He envisioned his death and became certain that he was going to be eaten up by beasts and wild animals. He thought that he would not be able to reach his destination. While these thoughts of despair were going on in his mind, he noticed his compassionate and powerful father standing before him. He freed him from his shackles and told him to ride and continue on his way and be careful of the enemies lying in wait on every corner along the way. His father told him, *as long as you are aware of the enemy and take precautions he will not be able to harm you, but when you become neglectful he will pounce on you. I am going ahead of you to the destination, so follow me.*

If this man was clever, sensible, intelligent and quick-witted, he would have resumed his journey afresh, more vigorously and with a faster pace. He would be cautious and prepared to combat the enemy. His second walk would be stronger and faster than the first one. He would be able to reach his destination quickly. However, if he became careless and ignored his enemy and returned to his previous condition without any better or worse, he will be as he was, and will be target of what he faced previously. If the incident caused slowness in his walk and he coveted that beautiful meadow and cold water and longed for them, his pace will be slower.

The second example is of a man who was in good health, but was affected by a sickness which required medicine for treatment. After taking the medicine, the harmful germs were removed and he returned to be healthier and in a stronger state than before. However, if his sickness caused more weakness and he was able to recover his strength, he would return to his previous condition. He would be less active if he failed to recover fully from his sickness. These two examples are sufficient for anyone who reflects on them.

Here is another example: A man left his house, intending to attend the prayer in the first row.

He walked without paying attention to anything then all of a sudden a man appeared, pulled at his clothes and stopped him for a while in order to prevent him from the prayer. Now this man has two options. He either engages with this man until he misses the prayer. This is the condition of the person who does not repent. Or he pulls himself away from the man and rescues himself to reach the prayer.

After this rescue he will have three options:
1. His walk is quick and fast in order to recover what he missed from that delay, and he may rush faster.
2. He resumes his walk at the same pace as before he was stopped.
3. The stop causes laziness in him and he misses the virtue of the first row, or the congregation or even the beginning of the prayer.

This is how the people who repent are, in their journey to Allah.

WHO IS BETTER: A MAN WHO NEVER COMMITTED A SIN OR THE ONE WHO COMMITTED A SIN THEN REPENTED?

Here is another important question: Is a man who was not involved in any act of disobedience of Allah better, or the one who committed an offence then turned to Allah in sincere repentance?

There is disagreement among the jurists on this issue. A faction is in favour of the one who did not disobey Allah at all over the one who repented sincerely. They argue this point in the following ways:

1. The best of the people and most perfect one is he who is most devoted to Allah. And this person who never committed an act of disobedience is the most devoted one and hence he is the best.

2. When the disobedient person was involved in offensive activities the devoted one went ahead of him by many stages. His rank became higher than the disobedient one. After repenting, the disobedient person resumed his journey and attempted to reach the devoted one, but he was too far ahead to catch up to him. They are like two people taking part in earning, whenever one of them had gained something, so did the other. One of them wasted his gain and refrained from continuing to earn, while the other continued earnestly in his work. If the careless person was moved by the fury of competition and resumed his work, he would find that his partner had amassed a great deal during this period of time. Anything he earned thereafter would then be similar to what his partner also earned, giving him no way to amass more and catch up. How could he then be equal to him?

3. The result of repentance is that the evils of the offender are erased and he becomes as though he did not perform them. His efforts in the period of committing sins are neither for him nor against him. How can his then efforts match the efforts of the person who continued earning and benefitting?

4. Allah, the Great, hates sinful deeds and violations of His commands. During the period of committing sins, this man was the subject of the anger of Allah, while the obedient man had His pleasure. The latter is definitely better than the one with whom Allah was pleased, then got angry then was pleased with him. Permanent pleasure is better than that which is interrupted by displeasure.

5. Sin is like poison and repentance is like its antidote, and obedience is like health and well being. Continuous health and well being is better than health interspersed with illness, or swallowing poison and then recovering. These could lead to his death or perpetual sickness.

6. The sinner would be in dire danger. His outcome could be any of three things: ruin and destruction by taking the poison; reduction of strength if no destruction takes place; or to return to the previous strength or even better. This last one is very rare. The sinner would then certainly be affected by the poison, with hope of being cured, unlike the obedient.

7. The devoted person had surrounded his garden of obedience with a strong fortress, which the enemies couldn't cross. His fruits, flowers and splendour were able to continuously flourish. The sinning man had opened a hole and made a gap in his building. The thieves and the enemies had a chance to enter from that opening and cause havoc everywhere. They destroyed its branches and ruined its walls. They cut off its fruits, burned its corners, cut the supply of the water and suspended its irrigation. How could this man then return to his previous condition? If his caretaker comes to help and mend what was ruined, opened the channels of water and rebuilt what was destroyed, then he will have either returned to his previous situation or to less than that, or perhaps slightly better. In any case he wouldn't have reached the status of the garden of his partner, which remained beautiful and continued growing further in its produce and freshness.

8. The enemy's interest in this rebellious man came from his lack of knowledge and the weakness of his resolve. That is why he is called ignorant. Allah, the Lord of the universe, said about Adam ﷺ, **"We found in him lack of determination."** *(20: 115)* He commanded His Messenger ﷺ, **"Be patient as were those of determination among the messengers."** *(46:35)* If a person who has strong determination, perfect knowledge and unshakable faith, his enemy will not be able to get access to him. He is in the best position.

9. The sin must produce bad effects, either in the form of complete annihilation or loss and

torment followed by forgiveness and entrance in Paradise, or a reduction in status or extinction of the lamp of the faith. The sinner will have been engaged in the removal of the traces of the sin and making atonement while the obedient one continued moving ahead in increasing his rank. For this reason the night prayer was especially ordered for the Prophet ﷺ because it raised his status, while for others it was to remove evil deeds. How can the two be compared?

10. The devoted person moved towards Allah with all his deeds. Whenever his good deeds increased, his reward increased. He is like a traveller who earned ten times more of what he had, taking another journey with his earnings and with the profits from the first trip, thus gaining another ten times more. He made a third trip with all this wealth and gained more, so on and so forth. If he felt exhausted at the end, he will have lost what he had gained, or even more. This is the meaning of what al-Junayd said, "If a true person walks towards Allah for one thousand years and then turns away from Him for a moment, he loses more than he had gained."

If this is the fate of a man who committed negligence then what will be the situation of the one who committed sins and got involved in disobedience?

A MAN WHO COMMITTED THE SIN THEN REPENTED IS BETTER

Another group preferred the person who committed a sin then repented, though they did not deny that the man who did not commit any sin has more good deeds. They put forward the following arguments:

1. The devotion by repentance is the dearest and most honourable to Allah. Allah loves those who constantly turn to Him in repentance. Had repentance not been the dearest matter to Allah, He would not have put His most honourable creature on trial by committing the sin. It was due to His love of His servant that He made him commit the sin so that he may turn to Him in repentance and thus raise his status Him. Allah has a special love for His repentant servants. This is illustrated further by the next point.

2. Repentance has a status with Allah Almighty which no other good deed has. That is why He, glory be to Him, feels the greatest pleasure when His servant turns to Him in repentance. It has been illustrated by the Prophet ﷺ by the happiness of a man who lost his camel which carried his food and drink in a dangerous desert, then found it. This type of happiness is not produced by any other good deed. This happiness has a great impact on the repentant person and his heart, which cannot be measured. This is the secret of decreeing the sin for servants. Through repentance, the servant achieves the rank of being loved and becomes beloved of Allah. Allah loves those who frequently turn to Him in repentance. This is explained further by the following point.

3. The devotion with repentance contains humility, submissiveness, adulation and dejection for Allah, which is dearer to Him than many physical exercises which may be more than the devotion of repentance. This is because the humility and submissiveness are the spirit of devotion.

4. The degree of humility and submission acquired by the repentant person is far higher than by any other person. It is because he shared the humility of need, devotion and love with the one who did not commit a sin, but surpassed him through the dejection of his heart because of the sin. Allah comes closer to His servant when his heart is broken and he feels humiliated. It is said in an Israeli report, "Where can I find you, my Lord?" He replied, "With those whose hearts have been broken because of Me." This is also proved by the report that the servant is nearest to Allah when he is in a position of prostration. It is because this is a position of humility and submission before his Lord. Pay attention to the statement of the Prophet ﷺ in his report from his Lord: "Allah, the Most High, will say on the Day of Judgement, 'Son of Adam, I asked you for food but you did not feed me.' The servant will say, 'How can I feed You when You are the Lord of the worlds?' Allah will say, 'My servant so-and-so asked you for food and you did not give it to him. Had you fed him you would have found it with Me. Son of Adam, I asked for drink and you did not provide Me with it.' The servant will say, 'How can I give You drink when You are the Lord of the worlds?' Allah will say, 'My servant so-and-so asked you for drink and you did not help him. Had you provided him with drink you would have found it with Me. Son of Adam, I fell sick and you did not come to see Me.' The servant will say, 'How can I visit You when You are the Lord of the worlds?' He will say, 'My servant so-and-so fell sick and you did not go to visit him. Had you gone to see him you would have found Me with him.'"

Consider the differences in the statements. In the case of a sick person Allah said, "You would have found Me with him," and in other cases He said, "You would have found it with Me." This is because a sick person's heart is broken no matter how strong he is. The illness breaks his heart. If he is a believer and his heart is broken, Allah is with him.

This may be the reason - and Allah knows better - for the granting of the supplications of three people: the oppressed, the traveller and the fasting person. Each one's heart is dejected. Being away from home for a traveller creates sadness in his heart. The same is true about fasting, which breaks the intensity of the animal side of the soul and subdues it. The point is that the candle of restoration, grace and bounty takes place in the candlestick of dejectedness and the repenting sinner has a big share of it. It could be further explained by the following point.

5. The sin connected with repentance may be more useful to the servant than many good deeds. This is the meaning of the saying of some early scholars that a servant commits a sin which takes him to Paradise, and does a good deed and ends up in Hell. He was asked, "How is that?" He replied, "The person committed a sin and it remained in front of his eyes when he

was standing or sitting or walking. He remembered his sin and felt dejected and regretful, so he repented and asked for forgiveness. This became the cause of his redemption. On the other hand, a person did a good deed and remembered it always while standing, sitting and walking. Whenever he remembered it he was filled with pride, conceit and vanity, thus causing his destruction. Sometimes a sin becomes the source of good deeds and spiritual conditions of the fear of Allah, feeling of shamefulness, bowing the head before Him in regret, crying, showing remorse and asking the Lord to overlook it. All these conditions are more useful for the servant than a good deed that creates a sense of arrogance, pride, contempt and looking down upon people. Surely this sin is more valuable to Allah and more likely to rescue the man than the good act of the person who is boastful of it and behaves as though he has done a favour to Allah. He may express sincerity, but Allah knows what is in his heart. If the people do not show respect to him and did not praise him, he may despise them. If he examines his soul thoroughly, he will discover that feeling hidden in it. If Allah wills good for this person, He will trap him in a sin to humiliate him and to let him know his status. In this way the Almighty will keep evil away from His servants and take out the illness of arrogance and pride from his heart. This sin is better to him than many good deeds. It is like taking medicine to treat an incurable disease. It resembles the story of Adam and his expulsion from Paradise for his mistake. As though it was said to him: *Adam, do not worry from the pain of the fault which is the cause of your shrewdness. It has taken out from you the disease with which you were not fit to remain with Us, and now you have been given the garment of servitude.*

Adam, I tried you with the sin because I wanted to show My bounty, generosity and grace to those who disobey Me. If you do not commit sins Allah will take you away and replace you with people who sin and then ask for forgiveness.

Adam, you came to Me like kings to kings, but now you will come to Me like the slaves to the kings.

Adam, if I were to protect you and your progeny from sin, then who I am going to show My magnanimity by My forbearance? Who I am going to grant My forgiveness and pardoning when I am the Most Relenting and Most merciful?

Adam, do not be distressed by My saying: "Get out of it". I have created you for it, but go down to the home of struggle, sow the seed of consciousness and water it from the clouds of eyes. When the plant becomes firm and stands on its stalk, come and reap it.

Adam, I did not expel you from the Garden but to make you beseech Me to come to it. I did not banish you from it but in order to make you return.

Adam, a sin which makes you humble to Us is more beloved to Us than a good deed which you feel proud of.

Adam, the moaning of the people is dearer to Us than the glorification of those who are conceited.

Son of Adam, as long as you call upon Me and put your hope in Me I will forgive whatsoever you did and I do not care. Son of Adam, if you come to Me with sins like the clouds and ask Me for forgiveness, I will forgive you. Son of Adam, if you meet Me with sins to fill the entire earth without associating any partner to Me, I will meet you with similar forgiveness.

It is said that a devoted person asked Allah to protect him from sin, whilst going round the Ka'bah. Then he slept and heard a voice saying, "You are asking for protection from sin and all My servants are asking for it. If I protect them then to whom will I show My forgiveness and generosity? Who I will turn to in order to accept their repentance? Son of Adam, if you believe in Me and do not associate a partner with Me, I will make the carriers of My Throne and those around it sing My praises and seek forgiveness for you while you are in your bed."

In the Divine Hadith reported by Abu Dharr Allah said:
"My servants, you are making mistake throughout the day and night and I forgive all the sins. Whoever knows that I have power to forgive, I forgive him and I do not care."

"Say (O Prophet): 'My servants who have harmed yourselves by your own excess, do not despair of Allah's mercy. Allah forgives all sins: He is truly the Most Forgiving, the Most Merciful." *(40:53)*

"My servant, do not lose hope. From you comes prayer and from Me the response. You seek forgiveness and I forgive. You repent and I will change your sins into good deeds."

6. The sixth argument is as follows. Allah said:
"Except those who repent, believe, and do good deeds: Allah will change the evil deeds of such people into good ones. Allah is Most Forgiving, Most Merciful." *(25:70)*

This is the greatest good tiding for the people who repent when their repentance is joined with belief and good deeds. This is the essence of repentance. Ibn Abbas said, "I never saw the Prophet ﷺ more pleased than when this verse was revealed." He then recited the following verse:
"Truly, We have given you a clear victory, so that Allah may forgive for you your past and future sins." *(48:1-2)*

Whether the change of evil deeds into good ones is going to take place in this world or in the Hereafter, there are two opinions among the scholars.

Ibn Abbas and his Companions said that it meant the change of their evil deeds into good ones here. So, their association of partners to Allah is changed into belief, their committing of adultery into chastity and purity, their lies into truthfulness and their betrayal into faithfulness.

The meaning of the verse in this case is that their evil characters and bad deeds are changed into beautiful characters and good deeds. It is like a person whose illness is changed into health, and a person afflicted by mishap into well being.

B. al-Musayyib and some other followers said that it means changing the evil deeds they did in the world into good ones on the Day of Resurrection. They will be given a good deed in place of every evil deed.

This second group supported their view by a report of al-Tirmidhi on the authority of Abu Dharr that the Messenger ﷺ said, "A man will be brought forward on the Day of Resurrection and it will be said, 'Present to him his minor sins and keep away the major ones.' He will be told, 'You did so-and-so on such-and-such day?' He will admit this and will be scared of the major sins. Then it will be said, 'Give him a good deed in place of every evil deed he did.' He will say, 'I do not see here sins which I committed.'"

After this, Abu Dharr said, "I saw the Messenger ﷺ laughing till his molars were seen."

The report is authentic but to argue on its basis has a problem. This person was punished for his evil deeds and was put in Hell and later was taken out of it and given good deed in place of every evil one. It was a favour from Allah Almighty. It does not indicate change of the sins into good deeds. Were it so, he would have not been punished, as the man who repented is not punished. The case here is of a man who repented and his sins were changed into good deeds. So this report does not serve the claim of those who have used it in the support of their case.

However, it can work in the argument after establishing a rule which will clear the way for argument. A sin must produce an effect. That effect is erased sometimes through repentance, sometime by good deeds that wipe it out, other times by the calamity that obliterates it, and by entering Hell to get rid of its impact. If the impact is very strong and the above mentioned matters were not enough to erase it then going to Hell becomes necessary. This is because there is no impurity and only those will enter it who are pure from every side. If any filth remains with anyone he is put in the bellow of purification so that the gold of his faith is cleansed from the dirt and then he will be eligible of admission into the house of the King.

When this is understood, it becomes clear that the impact of the sin is removed by sincere repentance, which is the strongest means. Sometimes it is removed after recovering the due and purification in the Fire. Once he is cleansed by the Fire and all traces of dirt are removed, he is given a good deed in place of every evil one. If he is cleansed by sincere repentance and traces of filth are removed, then he deserves to be given a good deed in place of every evil one. The removal of filth through sincere repentance is greater than cleansing by the Fire. Allah loves it. Sincere repentance is the real cause of cleansing and the Fire is only a substitute.

7. The person who repented has converted each of his evil deeds to good ones, through his regret. Regret is repentance, and repentance from every sin is a good deed. Through repentance every sin of his was replaced by good deeds. Now this good deed may be equal to the sin or less than that or more than that in importance. It depends on the sincerity of the repentance, truthfulness of the person and the devotion of the heart.

8. The sin of a person who is aware of Allah and His decree may bring more good deeds than the sin he committed. It may have produced enormous humility, fear and regret and brought greater benefit to him which he would not have been able to achieve if he was protected from that sin. He may have caused Satan so many worries, to the extent that he may have said, "I wish I would not have made him commit that mistake." Allah loves to see His servant causing disturbance and worry to Satan.

Pay attention to the statement of Allah: "Allah will change their sins into good deeds". He did not say that every evil deed will be replaced by a good deed. It is possible that one sin may be changed into many good deeds in accordance with the condition of the person.

As for the person mentioned in the Hadith, he did not change his sins into good deeds through sincere repentance and its requirements to earn many good deeds in place of one sin. So, he was given one good deed in place of every sin. The Messenger ﷺ did not say anything about the major sins but only smiled. However, the Hadith indicates that this change includes both the minor and the major sins in two ways:

Firstly, Allah said, "Hide from him the major sins". This is to inform that when the servant notices the change of minor sins, he hopes that the major ones also will be changed. His happiness with that will be greater and more gratifying.

Secondly, the Prophet ﷺ smiled at this point. His smile shows surprise at the favour which the servant receives and his admission of the sins he committed. He was only shown his minor mistakes but he confessed the major ones without being asked.

Blessed is Allah, the Lord of the worlds, the Most Generous of all, the Most Gracious of all, the Kind, the Compassionate, who shows His favour to His servant and covers him with all kinds of favours. There is no being worthy of worship except Him, the Most Beneficent, the Most Merciful.

THE SIGNIFICANCE OF FIRM INTENTION AND PREVENTION FROM FUTURE SINS

Many people define repentance as abandoning the sin, making a firm resolution of not committing the sin again and having remorse over what happened. If the offence involves another person then that is an additional matter which needs to be addressed. These are the conditions of repentance. Actually repentance as it occurs in the statements of Allah and His Messenger requires a firm intention of doing what is commanded and abiding by it. Only abandoning, firm intention and regret are not enough unless the determination for carrying out of the commands is found. This is the essence of repentance. It includes both matters. The essence of repentance is to turn to Allah with a commitment to do what is required and to abandon what is to be left. In this way it indicates turning from undesirable to desirable. Turning to what is desirable is one part of its meaning, and abandoning the undesirable is the other. Allah Almighty attached complete success to doing what is commanded and abandoning what is forbidden by repentance. He said:

"Turn to Allah in repentance, all of you, believers, so that you may succeed." *(24:31)*

Accordingly, every person who turns in repentance is successful and this depends on doing what is commanded and avoiding what is prohibited. Allah also said:

"Those who do not repent are wrongdoers." *(49:11)*

The person who does not carry out what is commanded is a wrongdoer, as much as the one who commits what is forbidden. He will be free from this offence when he repents, which includes both matters. The people are divided in to two categories only: Those who repent and those who do wrong. The ones who repent are those who:

"Turn to Allah in repentance, worship and praise Him, fast, bow down, and prostrate themselves, order what is good, forbid what is wrong and observe Allah's limits." *(9:112)*

Observing the limits of Allah is a component of repentance. Repentance includes all these matters and the person is regarded as turning to Allah in repentance when he turns to the commands of Allah and abandons His prohibitions, and deserts sinful acts in favour of obedience.

This shows that repentance is the core of the religion of Islam, and the man who turns to Allah in repentance is beloved to Allah as He has declared that He loves those who turn to Him and those who keep themselves clean. It is achieved by doing what is commanded and shunning what is prohibited.

Now it becomes clear that repentance means to abandon all that which Allah hates openly and secretly and do what He loves openly and secretly. This definition includes Islam, Iman and ihsan as well as all other spiritual stations. Repentance therefore is the final goal of a believer; it is the beginning and the end of his affairs. It is the objective for which the people are created. The most important part of it is to single out Allah as the only being worthy of worship.

Many people do not know the essence of repentance, let alone to fulfil its requirements in action and behaviour. Had repentance not been a comprehensive name of all the rules and regulations of Islam and the realities of faith, Allah would not have shown great happiness with the repentance of His servant.

SEEKING FORGIVENESS

Istighfar or seeking forgiveness is of two kinds: one that is not connected by repentance and the other connected by it. The example of the first kind is the advice of Noah to his people:
"Ask your Lord for forgiveness, He is Ever Forgiving. He will send down abundant rain from the sky for you." *(71:10-11)*

Salih said to his people:
"Why do you not ask Allah for forgiveness so that you may be given mercy." *(27:46)*

Allah commanded the people:
"Seek forgiveness of Allah; He is Most Forgiving, Most Merciful." *(2:199)*

Allah said about the hypocrites:
"Allah would not punish them while you (Prophet) are in their midst, nor would He punish them while they seek forgiveness." *(8:33)*

Asking forgiveness which is connected with repentance is in the following examples in the Qur'an:
"Ask your Lord for forgiveness, then turn to Him in repentance. He will grant you wholesome enjoyment until an appointed time and give His grace to everyone who has merit." *(11:3)*

The Prophet Hud said to his people:
"Ask forgiveness from your Lord, then repent to Him, He will send down rain for you in abundance from the sky." *(11:52)*

Salih said to his people:
"It was He who brought you into being from the earth and made you inhabit it, so ask forgiveness from Him and turn to Him in repentance. My Lord is near, and ready to answer." *(11:61)*

Shu'ayb said to his people:

"Ask forgiveness from your Lord, and turn to Him in repentance: my Lord is Merciful and Most Loving." *(11:91)*

Seeking forgiveness is like repentance, or rather, it is exactly repentance. It means seeking the forgiveness of Allah, to erase the sin and omit its trace and protect from its evil. It is not, as some people think, merely to cover. Allah covers those who ask forgiveness as well as those who do not. Covering is part of the meaning of forgiveness.

Its real notion is to protect from the evil of the sin and from it comes the word 'mighfar' (helmet) as it protects the head from harm. This type of seeking forgiveness is the one which holds back the punishment as mentioned in the statement of Allah:
"Allah would not punish them while they are seeking forgiveness." *(8:33)*

Allah does not punish a man who seeks forgiveness. As for a person who persistently commits the sin and asks for forgiveness, his asking forgiveness is not real and hence it is not going to prevent punishment. In short, seeking forgiveness includes repentance, and repentance includes asking for forgiveness. Both are closely connected. When they are joined together then seeking forgiveness refers to seeking protection from the evil of what has passed, and repentance means to turn and seek protection from the evil of sinful acts in future. So, there are two sins: one that has passed and the other which may be committed. Repentance is a firm intention of not doing it. Turning to Allah includes both matters: to ask Him to protect him from the evil consequence of what has been done and from the evil of the sinful acts he may do in future.

The sinner is like a man on a road which is leading to his destruction, and not taking him to his destination. He is commanded to turn from it and take the route which will take him to his salvation and to his destination where his success lies. In summary, there are two things: abandoning something and adopting another. Repentance is specifically to return to the right path and seeking forgiveness means to leave the evil way. When any of them is mentioned alone it includes both matters. That is why they occurred - and Allah knows better - in this order in Allah's statement:
"Seek forgiveness of your Lord then repent to Him." *(11:90)*

It is turning to the path of truth after deserting the way of falsehood.

Seeking forgiveness is from the category of removing harm and repentance is to seek benefit. Forgiveness means protection from the evil of the sin and repentance means to achieve after the protection what the servant loves. However, when any of them is mentioned alone it includes both matters.

THE TRUE ESSENCE OF SINCERE REPENTANCE

Allah said:

"You, who believe, turn to Allah in sincere repentance. Your Lord may well cancel your bad deeds for you, and admit you into Gardens graced with flowing streams." *(66:8)*

Here the Almighty has given protection from the evil of sins, through removing what the servant dislikes. He attached admission into Paradise to sincere repentance. The word 'Nasuh' in the case of repentance implies to make it free from any defect, flaw or corruption, and to make it complete from every side.

The early scholars explained this word in different ways but the sense is the same. 'Umar b. al-Khattab and Ubayy b. Ka'b said, "Sincere repentance refers to repent from the sin and not to return to it again as the milk does not return to the udder." Hasan al-Basari explained it by saying that it means that the servant is regretful for what happened and resolves not to do it again.

Muhammad b. Ka'b al-Qurazi said, "Sincere repentance combines four things: Seeking forgiveness by the tongue, refraining from evil by the body, having intention in the heart of not returning to it again and deserting the bad associates."

As a matter of fact sincerity of repentance includes three things:
1. To repent from all sins, not leaving out a single one;
2. To have a firm and true intention so that there remains no hesitation or reluctance and having the aim and objective of abandoning the sinful act;
3. To make it clean from any defect or blemish and make it purely for the fear of Allah and desire of gaining His reward and keeping away from His punishment. It should not be aimed at saving one's honour, position, worldly possessions or protection of power and wealth or receiving praise from the people or because of being incapable, or any other matter which will make repentance incorrect and insincere.

The first of those three matters relates to the acts from which the servant repents. The second one is connected with the one to whom he turns and the third one is connected with the person himself. When repentance is made with sincerity, and from all sins, it will include seeking forgiveness and it will wipe out all the sins. This is the perfect repentance.

It is Allah whose help is sought, on Him we put our trust and there is no power nor strength except with Him.

THE DIFFERENCE BETWEEN REMOVING MISDEEDS AND FORGIVING SINS

Allah the Glorious has mentioned them together and sometimes separately from one another. He mentioned them together in the following verse in the supplication of His believing servants:

"Our Lord, forgive us our sins and remove our misdeeds and cause us to die with the righteous." *(3:193)*

He cited removing the misdeeds alone in the following verse:

"Those who believe and do righteous deeds and believe in what has been sent down upon Muhammad – and it the truth from their Lord – He will remove from them their misdeeds and amend their condition." *(47:2)*

The Almighty said about forgiving sins:

"They will have in it (Paradise) fruit of every kind and forgiveness from their Lord." *(47:15)*

"Our Lord, forgive us our sins and our excesses in our affairs." *(3:147)*

So, here are four matters: sins, misdeeds, forgiveness and removal.

Sins refer to the major ones and misdeeds refer to the minor ones. The latter can be removed by expiation, which does not work with major sins. The evidence that misdeeds are minor sins which are wiped out is in the following statement of Allah Almighty:

"If you avoid the major sins which you are forbidden, We will remove from you your minor misdeeds and admit you to a noble entrance." *(4:31)*

It is reported in the Sahih of Muslim on the authority of Abu Hurayrah that the Messenger of Allah ﷺ said, "Five prayers, Friday to next Friday, Ramadan to next Ramadan are expiation for the misdeeds between them as long as the major sins are avoided."

The word 'maghfirah' (forgiving) is more comprehensive than the word 'nukaffir' (removing). The former is used for major sins and the later for minor misdeeds. Forgiveness includes protection and safeguarding while removing indicates covering and elimination. However, when they are used alone they imply both meanings. When Allah said the following, He included both major and minor sins:

"He removed from them their misdeeds." *(47:2)*

This explains the secret behind the promise of removal of misdeeds, and not forgiveness for calamities, sorrows, distress, weariness and discomfort as the Messenger ﷺ said, "No worry or distress or any other trouble, even the piercing of a thorn, which a believer suffers from but Allah removes from him his misdeeds."

Suffering alone cannot remove the major sins, they can be wiped out by repentance or plenty of good deeds which can cover the sins. They become like the sea that does not change even if there are rotten corpses in it. In the world, the sinful people have three big rivers in which to cleanse themselves. If this was not enough then their cleaning will be done in the river of Hell on the Day of Resurrection. These rivers that remove the sins are sincere repentance, enough good deeds to overwhelm the sins and a lot of suffering. When Allah wills good for a servant, He admits him in one of those three rivers, and he will arrive clean on the Day of Judgement and will not need a fourth cleansing.

ALLAH RESPONDS TO THE REPENTANCE OF A SERVANT

Repentance of the servant is surrounded by grace and guidance before he turns to Allah in repentance, and after he repents. His repentance is encircled between two bounties of Allah. Allah turns to him first by opening the door of repentance, supporting him and putting the thought of it in his mind. As a result he turns to Allah in repentance and Allah shows His grace to him by accepting his repentance and rewarding him. Allah said:

"Allah Has relented towards the Prophet, the emigrants and helpers who followed him in the hour of adversity when some hearts almost wavered. In the end He relented towards them; He is Most Kind and Merciful to them. And He relented to the three men who stayed behind: when the earth, for all its spaciousness, closed in around them, when their very souls closed in around them, when they realised that the only refuge from Allah was with Him, He relented towards them in mercy in order for them to return to Him. Allah is indeed Ever Relenting, the Most Merciful." *(9:117-118)*

In these verses Allah declared that He turned to them before they turned to Him in repentance, and that turning with help from Him made them repent. It was He who guided and helped them to turn to their Lord in repentance. It is like the guidance of the servant by Allah before he was guided. He chose the right path by the guidance of Allah and as such he achieved double guidance and was rewarded for both of them. Allah said:

"He has increased the guidance of those who follow the right path." *(47:17)*

He guided them and they followed the right path and then He guided them again. It is the opposite of what happened with the people of deviation, as Allah said:

"When they deviated, Allah caused their hearts to deviate."*(61:5)*

The second deviation is the punishment of their first deviation.

This act of Allah reveals the secret of His two names: 'the First' and 'the Last'. He is the One who prepares and then gives support. From Him comes cause. He is the One who gives protection from Himself as the most knowledgeable person about Him said: "I seek refuge in You from

You." The servant turns and Allah turns too. The turning of the servant is to come back to his master after running away from him, and the turning of Allah is of two kinds: sanction and assistance, and acceptance and success.

THE BEGINNING AND THE END OF REPENTANCE

Repentance has a beginning and an end. Its beginning is to turn to Allah by taking His straight path which He has set out for His servants to achieve His pleasure. He ordered to follow it.

"This is My path which is straight, so follow it, and do not follow other ways." *(6:153)*

"You (Muhammad) give guidance to the straight path, the path of Allah, to Whom belongs all that is in the heavens and earth." *(42: 52-53)*

"They were guided to good speech and to the path of the One Worthy of Praise." *(22:24)*

The end of repentance is to return to Allah in the Hereafter and take the path He has set to His Paradise. Anyone who turned to Allah in this world in repentance, He will turn to him in the Hereafter with reward. It is one of the interpretations of the Almighty's saying:
"Anyone who repents and does good deeds truly returns to Allah." *(25:71)*

Al-Baghawi and other commentators said, "The meaning is that he will return to Allah after death in a good position, better than others."

The first is turning from disbelief and the second is turning to Allah for reward and recompense.

Another interpretation is that whoever has a firm intention of repenting, he should make it purely for the sake of Allah not for any other reason.

The third interpretation is that the repenting person should look to whom he is repenting. His repentance and turning should only be to Allah.

The fourth meaning of the verse is that repentance starts with intention, and when it becomes firm, decisive repentance ensues. The first repentance in the verse refers to the intention and the second one to its execution. So the meaning will be that anyone who makes his mind to turn to Allah in repentance, he has to prove it through actions.

CHAPTER FIVE
CATEGORISATION OF SINS

THE DIVISION OF SINS INTO MAJOR AND MINOR

Sins are divided into major and minor. Allah, the Most High said:

"If you avoid major sins you have been forbidden, We shall wipe out your minor misdeeds and let you in through the entrance of honour." *(4:31)*

"Those who avoid major sins and foul acts, though they may commit minor sins: your Lord is ample in forgiveness." *(53:31)*

"Far better and more lasting is what Allah will give to those who believe and trust in their Lord, who shun major sins and gross indecencies." *(42:36-37)*

The Messenger of Allah ﷺ said, "Five daily prayers, Friday prayer to the next Friday, fast of Ramadan to the next Ramadan are the source of erasing the sins committed between them, provided the major sins are avoided."

The early scholars have disagreed concerning the number of major sins. Abdullah b. 'Amr related, as recorded in two Sahihs, that the Messenger of Allah ﷺ said, "Major sins are the association of partners with Allah, disobedience to parents, killing a person and making false oaths."

Abu Bakrah narrated that the Messenger of Allah ﷺ said, "Shouldn't I tell you about the gravest sins?" The Companions said, "Yes, tell us, Messenger of Allah." The Prophet ﷺ said, "They are the association of partners with Allah and the disobedience of parents." He was reclining, then he sat up and added, "And telling lies." He continued repeating it till we said, "If he would stop."

It is also reported in the Sahih on the authority of Abdullah b. Mas'ud who said, "I asked the Messenger of Allah, which sin is greater?" He replied, "That you assign a partner to Allah while He has created you." I asked, "Then which one?" The Messenger replied, "That you kill your child for the fear that he will share your food." "Then which one comes next?" I enquired, and the Messenger said, "That you commit adultery with your neighbour's wife."

Then the following verse was revealed in confirmation of what the Messenger ﷺ said:
"Who never invoke other deity beside Allah, nor take life, which Allah has made sacred, except in pursuit of justice, nor commit adultery." *(25:68)*

Another report from Abu Hurayrah in two Sahihs says the Messenger of Allah ﷺ said, "Keep away from seven destructive characters." The Companions asked, "What are they, Messenger of Allah?" He replied, "Attributing partners to Allah, practicing sorcery, taking the life which Allah has made sacred except in the pursuit of justice, use of usury, consumption of the wealth of an orphan, running away on the day of combat, and accusing chaste innocent believing women." Abdullah b. 'Amr related that the Messenger of Allah ﷺ said, "It is the gravest sin that a person should abuse his parents."

The Companions asked, "How can a person abuse his parents?" The Messenger replied, "He abuses a man's father who in retaliation abuses his father, and he abuses a man's mother who abuses his mother."

Abu Hurayrah narrated that the Messenger of Allah ﷺ said, "Among the gravest sins for a Muslim is to attack the honour of his Muslim brother without a just cause."

Abdullah b. Mas'ud said, "The gravest sins are: association of partners with Allah, feeling secure against Allah's plan, despairing Allah's mercy and losing hope in Allah's help."

Sa'id b. Jubayr said that a man asked Abdullah b. Abbas about the grave sins and asked, "Are they seven?" Ibn Abbas replied, "they are close to seven hundred. However, there is no grave sin with seeking forgiveness and no minor sin with persistency." He further said, "Any act by which Allah has been disobeyed is a major sin. Whoever commits that should ask for forgiveness of Allah. Allah is not going to put a man in Fire for ever except the one who has denounced Islam or rejects to acknowledge an obligatory act or denies the fate."

Abdullah b. Mas'ud said that all that which Allah has mentioned in the chapter of women are major sins:
"If you avoid the grave sins that you have been forbidden, We will wipe out your minor sins." *(4:31)*

Ali b. Abu Talha said, "Major sin is that which Allah threatened with Fire or anger, or curse or punishment."

Al-Dahhak defined the major sin as being that about which Allah fixed a punishment in the world or torment in the Hereafter.

Al-Husayn b. al-Fadl said that it is all those acts which Allah has called 'big' or 'great' as in the following verses:
"It (i.e. consuming the property of orphans with one's own) is a great sin." *(4:2)*

"Their (i.e. the children's) killing is a big offence." *(17:31)*

"Association of partners with Allah is great injustice." *(31:13)*

"Your treachery is truly great." *(12:28)*

"Glory be to You! This is a great slander." *(24:16)*

"This is to Allah a great (offence)." *(33:53)*

Sufyan al-Thawri said, "Major sin is the wrong which happened between you and other people and minor is the one which is between you and Allah. It is so because Allah is Generous and He pardons." To support his statement, he quoted the Hadith of Anas b. Malik that the Messenger of Allah ﷺ said, "A caller will call from the side of the Throne on the Day of Judgement, 'The Community of Muhammad, Allah, the Most High, has forgiven you all, the believing men and women. So, now you settle your wrongdoings between you, and enter Paradise by My mercy.'

I say that Sufyan means that the sins which are between the servant and Allah are easier than offences concerning human beings. The sins committed by a man regarding Allah's rights may be wiped out by seeking forgiveness, pardoning, and intercession and so on. However, the misdeeds among the people must be fully settled. Al-Tabarani related in his Mu'jam that the Messenger of Allah ﷺ said, "Injustice will be divided into three categories on the Day of Judgement, one which Allah will not forgive and that is the association of others with Allah".

He then recited:
"Allah will not forgive association of others with Him." *(4:48)*

The second category is that which Allah will not leave anything of it. It is the misbehaviour of people with one another and the third one is that which Allah does not care and that is the wrongdoing of the servant concerning the duties regarding Allah."

It is known that this last category includes major and minor sins. However, the one who is concerned with them is the most Generous one. What He relinquishes of His right and grants is much more than He exacts. This matter is easier from the one which He is not going to leave because of His justice and will give the right of everyone to him.

Malik b. Mighwal said, "Major sins are the sins of the people of innovation while the minor sins are the mistakes of the people of the Sunnah."

I say that he wants to say that innovation is one of the major sins and it is greater than the grave sins of the followers of the Sunnah. The major sins of the followers of the Sunnah are small compared to the innovations. This is the sense of the statement of an early scholar that innovation is more beloved to the Devil than sin because there is no repentance from innovation while there is an opportunity to repent from a sin.

According to some other scholars major sin is the one which is committed deliberately, while the minor is the one which is committed by mistake or forgetfulness or under duress. It also includes the thoughts which comes to mind at the time of committing the sin. This has been pardoned for this community.

I say here that this is the weakest statement because mistakes and forgetfulness or being forced do not come under the category of sinning. As far as sins committed deliberately are concerned they could be either major or minor.

Another definition was that major sins are those which were committed but considered alright, such as the sin of Satan, while minor sins are the mistakes of those who ask for forgiveness, such as the mistakes of Adam.

I say that the sin of the one who does not bother about its gravity revolves between disbelief and interpretation. If he knows that it is unlawful, then he is unbeliever. If he is not aware of its prohibition then he is either an interpreter or an imitator. When a person seeks forgiveness, his sincere and perfect supplication will wipe out both his major and minor sins. No sin remains with seeking forgiveness.

This definition is also weak unless it is said that the sin of a man who has knowledge of its being forbidden is greater than the sin of the one who is aware of prohibition and regrets and seeks forgiveness.

Al-Suddi said, "The major sins are those which Allah has prohibited and the minor ones are their preliminaries and their results which are shared by both the good and bad persons. They are for example gazing, touching, kissing etc. He supported his view by the following statement of the Prophet ﷺ, "The eyes commit adultery and the feet commit adultery, but it is the private organ which makes it true or false."

Another definition is that major sins are those which the people regard as little and the minor ones are those which they consider big and fear to commit them. The people who give this meaning support their view by a report in Sahaih of al-Bukhari that Anas ﷺ said, "You do things which seem to you thinner than hair while we used to regard them in the time of the Messenger of Allah, may the blessing and peace of Allah be on him, among the most serious sins."

Al-Suddi's statement that the major sins are those which are forbidden by Allah, is defining a matter by it. He may have the intention of saying that forbidden acts are of two types: That which contains evil and committing the source of an evil. This is certainly a major sin, such as taking a life, stealing, falsely accusing someone and committing adultery.

The second one is that which is preliminary of the offence like gazing, touching, conversation and kissing. These are minor sins. So, minor sins are preliminary and the major one is the objective and the end.

CORRECT UNDERSTANDING OF THE MAGNITUDE OF SINS

Regarding the definition that what the people consider little is major and what they consider big is minor, it is not correct. The servant regards the gazing as little and considers the immoral act big. However, if the intention is that considering the offence small makes it big to Allah, and considering it big makes it small, then it is correct. When an offence is taken to be little by the servant, it becomes major to Allah. On the other hand when a sin is taken to be serious it becomes small to Him. The Hadith gives this meaning. The Companions considered these acts serious and destructive due to their perfect status to Allah, but later generations consider these acts small because of their low status.

If you would like to understand it, look at the attitude of the Companions. When they heard a statement from the Messenger of Allah 轟 did they raise objections to it on the basis of their analogies, tastes, reasons, inclinations or emotions? Allah saved them from this type of behaviour. Umar b. Al-Khattab ruled for the man who preferred his judgement on the statement of the Messenger 轟 to be killed. What would he have done if he saw what we are witnessing today? People prefer the opinion of every man over the ruling of the infallible Prophet. Allah's help is sought and to Him we must return.

Another group said that a major sin is the association of partners with Allah and that which leads to it, while a minor sin is that of the people of Tawhid. They based their view on the following verse:
"Allah does not forgive the joining of partners with Him; anything less than that He forgives to whoever He will." *(4:48)*

They also quoted the Divine Hadith in which Allah says:
"Son of Adam, if you meet Me with the sins to fill the entire world and you come without joining partners to Me, I will meet you with the same amount of forgiveness."

They also quoted the Hadith cited earlier concerning the three categories of sins. However, their argument carries no weight. The Qur'anic verse quoted by them indicates the difference between the shirk and other sins. It asserts that shirk is not going to be pardoned without repentance, however, the other sins are left with the will of Allah. It shows that all other sins are below shirk. It is true, if this is what the advocates of this definition mean, then there is no dispute about it. But if they want to say that all sins other than shirk are minor then it is rejected.

A question may be asked here: if shirk and other sins can be erased with repentance, then what is the difference between shirk and others sins? Does it apply to both the person who repents and the one who does not? Or one of them belongs to the person who repents and the other to the one who does not? What is difference between this verse and the following saying of Allah Almighty?

"Say: My servants who have harmed yourselves by your own excess, do not despair of Allah's mercy. Allah forgives all sins: He is truly the Most Forging, the Most Merciful." *(39:53)*

The answer is that each of the above verses concern one group. The one of Qur'anic chapter 9 is about those who do not repent. It is borne by the fact that it differentiated between shirk and other sins as regards forgiveness. It is clear in the religion of Islam that shirk is forgiven by repentance, otherwise the Islam of a disbeliever could never be considered correct.

Moreover, it restricted the forgiveness of sins other than shirk to those He wanted. The forgiveness of the people who repent is general without any restriction. That shows the above verse to be about the one who does not repent.

As for the verse 39:53, which reads that "Allah forgives all the sins", it applies to the repentant because it is general and not restricted to some and not limited with any sin. It is known that He does not forgive disbelief and there are many other sins which He will not forgive. It means that this general rule applies to the repentant. Consequently whoever repents from any sin will be forgiven.

As the above Divine Hadith says, "(My servants), if you come to Me with sins full of earth and you come without associating any partner with Me, I will meet you with similar forgiveness".

It does not indicate that all sins besides shirk are minor, it only tells us that whoever does not commit shirk all his sins will be forgiven no matter how many they are. However, one has to keep in mind the attachment of the faith with the actions, otherwise the purpose of the statement of the Messenger of Allah ﷺ will not be understood and confusion will arise.

You should know that the act of not associating any partner with Allah cannot come from a person who persistently commits sins. It is impossible for a person who insists on committing grave sins and the one who persists on committing minor ones to have sincere Tawhid. Do not pay attention to a man who is bent on arguing and has no share of inner feeling. As a result his heart has become hard like stone or even harder. He may say: 'What is wrong? Why is it impossible? If it happens nothing outrageous will occur.'

Leave this confused person with his ignorance and remember that the source of the insistence on the sin is the fear of others besides Allah. He loves others besides Allah, submits to him and puts his trust in him and thus is drowned in the oceans of shirk. This could be known by the man himself if he has power of reasoning. The disgrace of offence sticks to the heart and produces fear of others besides Allah. This is exactly an act of shirk. This brings forth the love for other than Allah and makes the person seek help from other sources to achieve his aim. In this way his act is not for Allah, and this is the essence of shirk. It is possible that he believes, like Abu Jahl and the worshippers of idols, in the tawhid of *rububiyya* and acknowledges that there is no creator except Allah. However, this is not enough. It is not enough to save the worshippers of the idols. *Tawhid al-ilahiyya* is the distinctive factor between the polytheists and the monotheists.

The point is that a person who did not associate any partner with Allah will never meet Allah with sins full of the earth, without repentance. He believes in pure oneness of Allah with love and submission. He is full of humility for Him, fears and loves only Allah Almighty.

Regarding the Hadith of the categories, it indicates that Allah does not mind if His rights are neglected. He does not bother as much about it as He bothers about the rights of His servants, but it does not mean that He is not going to censure at all, or all that was committed is minor. It means only that Allah, the Most High, acts with leniency, kindness and pardon about His rights much more than He will do with the rights of human beings. This shows that all the arguments forwarded by them are not valid. Allah knows best.

Some people believe that the minor sins are those for which no punishment is prescribed in the world or the Hereafter. Any sin for which there is a prescribed punishment in the worldly life such as adultery, drinking wine, theft and accusation, or there is stern warning of torment in the Hereafter such as consuming the wealth of an orphan, drinking in the vessels of gold and silver, suicide, treachery and so on, are all among the major sins. Ibn Abbas spoke truthfully when he said that the major sins were close to seven hundred rather than seven.

There is a point here which should be understood. A major sin may be accompanied by shame, fear and thought of it being major, which then makes it a minor one. On the other hand, a minor sin which is accompanied with lack of shame, fear, and indifference and thinking it little can make it become a major sin, and even worse than the major sins. This is something which is connected with the heart and is beyond mere acting. Human beings recognise it in themselves and in others. It is also to be noted that the shortcoming of a lover and the one who has been doing good deeds is forgiven and written off, which is not done to others.

I heard Shaykh al-Islam Ibn Taymiyyah, may Allah sanctify his soul, say, "Look at Moses, may Allah's blessing and peace be on him, he threw the tablets which contained the words of Allah, which He wrote by His hand, and broke them. He also dragged a prophet like him i.e. Harun, by his beard, and slapped the angel of death and gouged his eye. He went further to complain to his Lord about raising the status of Muhammad, may Allah's blessing and peace be on him, on the night of the nocturnal journey. Allah, the Most High, tolerated all of this and showed His love and honour for him. He (Moses) earned this honour because he stood firm for the sake of Allah before His greatest enemy, carried out His commands and faced severe problems in dealing with the Copts and the Children of Israel. So, his aforementioned behaviour compared to his exemplary works resembles a hair in the sea.

Look at Jonah (Yunus), the son of Matthew, who did not reach that position of Moses - when he offended his Lord once, He dealt with him severely and imprisoned him in the belly of the whale. The Almighty did not condone for him as He did for Moses. Here there is the difference between a person who committed one sin and had no deposit of good deeds, which can plead for him, and another who when he committed a mistake, his good deeds provided all the sources of excuse.

A poet once said, "When a beloved commits an offence, his good deeds produce thousand of intercessors."

The good acts plead for their people to Allah. They make them remember Him if he is surrounded by troubles. Allah, the Most High said about the man of the whale (Jonah):
"If he had not been one of those who glorified Allah, he would have stayed in its belly until the Day when all are raised up." *(37:143-144)*

But since Pharaoh had not done good deeds which could plead for him, and he said:
"I believe there is no god except the one that the Children of Israel believe in." *(10:90)*

Jibril said to him:
"Now? When you had always been rebel, and a troublemaker!" *(10:91)*

According to a report in the Musnad, the Messenger of Allah ﷺ said, "All those words you utter concerning the glorification, exaltation and praise to express the glory of Allah, they gather around the Throne. They hum like the humming of the bee. They remember those who utter them. Wouldn't one of you love to be remembered in that way?"

It shows that anyone whose good deeds overwhelm his evil deeds will be successful and will not be punished. His evil deeds will be erased because of his good deeds. This is how the mistakes of a person who confessed the oneness of Allah is forgiven, while the sins of the person involved in association of partners with Allah are not. The believer in the oneness of Allah has done what Allah loves and for that reason he deserves to be pardoned and treated in a different way from an individual who has committed shirk. It is in accordance with the power of the belief of the man. The person whose belief is greater and more sincere, Allah's forgiveness for him will be more complete. Consequently, if a person meets Allah without associating any object with Allah, all his sins will be forgiven no matter how many they are.

It is not to say that no one from the people of Tawhid is going to Hell. There will be a good number of them who will go to Hell for their sins and will suffer in accordance with their offences and then will be taken out. There is no contradiction between the two things for a person who pays attention to what we have said. However, we would like to make it clearer due to its importance and the need of the people to understand it.

Remember that the rays of the words 'there is no god except Allah' shatter the clouds and mists of the sins in accordance with the power or weakness of the rays. The people are different in this light so much that is known only to Allah, glory be to Him. The light of this statement shines like the sun in some people's hearts. Others have its light like a glittering star, and others have it like a big torch. Some have it like shining lamp and others like a weak lamp.

This light will appear on the Day of Judgement before the believers and to their rights in line with the light of this statement in their hearts in knowledge, practice and position. The intensity and brightness of this light burn the darkness of the suspicion and desire to the extent that no doubt or desire remains. This is the condition of the true believer in the oneness of Allah, who did not associate any partner to Him. Any sin or desire or doubt that approaches this light is destroyed. The heaven of his belief is protected by stars from any thief who attempts to steal his good deeds. The thief can succeed only in the condition of carelessness which every human being experiences. When this man wakes up and realises that something has been taken away from him, he recovers it or gains more than what was taken. This is his situation with the thieves among Jinn and mankind. He is not like the one who has the door of his treasury unprotected and left it open for the plunderers.

It is to be remembered that Tawhid is not only to confess that there is no creator beside Allah, who is the Lord and Master of everything, as the worshippers of the idols used to declare even though they were polytheists. Tawhid requires the love of Allah, submission and full obedience to Him. It also means to worship Him with sincerity and to seek His pleasure in all actions and words, in giving and holding, loving and hating. It should be so all-encompassing that it leaves to chance the motives of sins and insistence on them. If a person understands this, he will be able to understand the meaning of the statement of the Messenger of Allah ﷺ, "Allah has prohibited the Fire on any one who says "There is no god except Allah," and seeks the pleasure of Allah by it."

He will be able to understand the following words of the Prophet 鸞, "Whoever says 'there is no god except Allah.'"

He will be able to understand many other statements which many people find difficult to comprehend and which were taken to be nullified. Others thought that they were spoken before the obligations and prohibitions were given. Others considered them to apply to the fire of disbelievers and polytheists. Many people interpreted them to mean that such person will not remain in Hell for ever. All these are unacceptable explanations.

The Messenger 鸞 did not mean that salvation could be achieved by uttering the testimony with tongue alone. It is against the teachings of Islam. The hypocrites said it, yet they will be placed in the lowest part of Hell. It is, therefore, a combination of saying by the heart and by the tongue together. Saying by heart means to understand it, to be certain about it and to realise the essence of what it contains. That is the negation and affirmation and knowing the essence of the Divine nature of Allah which is purely for Him and not for anyone else. This belief must be established in the heart with knowledge, realisation and certainty. Only then the person can be saved from Hell. Any statement with which the Messenger has attached reward is this type of statement. For example he said, "Whoever says *subhanallahi wa bihamdihi* (glory is to Allah and praise is for Him) one hundred times, his sins will be wiped out even if they are like the froth of the sea".

This cannot be achieved by uttering with the tongue alone. However, if a man says it with his tongue, unmindful of its meaning and not trying to contemplate its contents, and his heart is not in conformity with his tongue, nor if he knows its real importance and still hopes to be rewarded, his sins will be forgiven in accordance with what he has in his heart. Actions are graded because of what is in the hearts of the people. It could be that two acts are the same but there is big difference between them, such as the distance between heaven and the earth. Two men perform the prayer but their prayers are very different.

Look attentively at the report of the card which will be put in one side of the scale against ninety-nine registers, each one as big as the range of vision, and the card turns out to be heavy and the registers are flown away and the man is not punished. It is known that every believer in the oneness of Allah has that card, and many of them will go to Hell for their sins. The secret which made the card of that person heavier than those records is his understanding of the testimony. Others did not have that and they ended up in Hell.

If you need more clarification, then look at the man whose heart is filled with your love and the one who is unmindful and has no concern about you. His heart is engaged with the love of others whom he puts above your love. Will the remembrance of these two be equal? Consider the position of your two children, two slaves and two wives with this attitude. Will you consider them to be equal?

Also pay attention to what the realities of faith which the murderer of a hundred people realised in his heart, and did not hinder his walk to the village. He collapsed with his chest to the side of the village of good people. It was that sincere belief that he was considered among the people of the town and rescued.

Similar to this is the case of the prostitute who noticed a dog suffering from the intense thirst and licking the mud, she had no means to fetch water and did not have the intention of showing off - yet she went down the well, filled her socks with water and saved the animal. She did not think of the risk for her own life. She filled her socks with water and held them by her mouth in order to climb up and show mercy to this creature, which other people would disregard and strike. She did not expect any thanks or recompense from it. The light of this much *Tawhid* burnt down all her sins of the past and she was forgiven.

This is how acts and people are judged by Allah. Nevertheless many people are heedless of this, which is like a chemical elixir that when a very small amount of which is put on a tremendous amount of copper can turn it into gold. Allah's help is sought.

It is said that a beloved person is treated much more kindly than a hateful person, and a close friend's mistakes are condoned unlike others. In the same way a learned person's shortcomings are ignored, unlike those of an ignorant. Al-Tabarani has reported that the Prophet ﷺ said, "When Allah, glory be to Him, will gather the mankind on a common ground, He will say to the learned people, 'I was worshipped according to your verdict, and I knew that you made mistakes like other people. However, I did not put My knowledge with you to punish you. Go - I have forgiven you.'"

It is the requirement of wisdom, generosity and benevolence, but what will you say about the double punishment which has been mentioned about them if they commit unacceptable acts? For example Allah, the Most High said:
"Wives of the Prophet, if any of you does something clearly outrageous, she will be doubly punished." *(33:30)*

"(Prophet), if We had not made you stand firm, you would almost have inclined a little towards them. In that case We would have made you taste a double punishment in this life, and a double punishment after death and you would have found no one to help you against Us." *(17:74-75)*

Allah also said:
"If he (the Prophet) had attributed some fabrication to Us, We would certainly have seized his right hand and cut off his lifeblood." *(69:44-46)*

Allah Almighty gave a stern warning to His beloved Prophet, but protected him from inclining to His enemies and from fabricating. There are many others who incline to His enemies and attributing fabrications to Him, but He gives them respite and does not bother about them. These are the people of innovation and speaking wrong about His names and attributes.

What was said earlier about Jonah belongs to this area. He was not forgiven for his anger and had to be kept in the belly of the whale. The case of the father of the mankind is enough in this case. He was not pardoned for a little sin and was thrown out of Paradise. The answer is, that is also right, and there is no contradiction between the two matters. A man to whom Allah's full grace is granted and who has been singled out by special gifts of the Almighty, and who has been honoured by Him and brought nearer and placed in the position of a beloved person, his status requires that he should be protected from the slightest doubt and confusion. Such a person is so keen on safeguarding his obedience to Allah and putting His pleasure over everything else that he deserves to be taken full care of by his Master and enjoy a greater portion of His grace. His responsibility is more than anyone else's. If he is heedless and fails to fulfil his duties of his high rank, he is reminded in a way which is not available for a person who is not so close. Still his mistakes are condoned and he is treated in a different way from others. In this way the two matters gather concerning him.

If you want to know the meeting of the two matters and there being no contradiction between them, just look at the situation around you. A king overlooks the offences of his special friends and close allies and treats them in a different way to others. We have cited examples of both cases and cleared that there is no contradiction between them.

Here is another clarification: If you have two slaves or two children or two wives, and one of them is more beloved to you and you like him more and treat him more affectionately, both matters are found in your treatment. You treat him in accordance with your love and admiration. When you consider your kind treatment and perfect care, you treat him in a different way and draw his attention to his shortcoming. When you look at his love, sincerity, service and complete devotion to you, you tend to forgive his mistakes, which you do not do with others. The two treatments are in accordance with your act and his acts.

This meaning is clear in the ruling of the Shari'ah, concerning the punishment of adultery and fornication. It has prescribed stoning to death for a man who was honoured with marriage but transgressed its boundary. But only striking was prescribed for a person who was not married. Again the punishment was full in the case of a man who enjoyed freedom but half on a person who was a slave and owned by another man.

Glory is to the One whose wisdom concerning His creatures and judgement astonished the reasons of the learned men and is the best evidence that He is the Greatest Judge.

CHAPTER SIX
CATEGORY OF OFFENCES THAT NEED REPENTANCE

There are twelve categories the servant is required to get rid of, to be called repentant. These are cited in the Book of Allah and listed below:

1. Disbelief
2. Association of partners with Allah
3. Hypocrisy
4. Transgression
5. Disobedience
6. Sinning
7. Hostility
8. Immorality
9. Abomination
10. Oppression
11. Speaking about Allah without knowledge
12. Following a path other than that of the believers

These twelve categories all revolve around that which Allah has prohibited. Most people are involved in them except the followers of the Messengers, may Allah's blessings and peace be upon them. A person may be caught up by all of them or most of them or some of them or even only one. He may know it or may not be aware of it. Sincere repentance is to be free of them and take caution against committing them. However, getting rid of them is possible only for someone who knows them.

We are going to speak about them and mention the areas in which they meet and differ. In this way their limits and realities will be recognised. Allah is a supporter in all of this, just how He helps in other matters. There is no power, no strength, except with Allah.

This part is the most valuable of this book and the servant is in great need of it.

DISBELIEF
Disbelief (kufr) is of two types: major and minor.

Major disbelief will result in staying in Hell for ever. Minor disbelief cause the fulfilment of the threat not of abiding forever. The Messenger ﷺ said: "Two matters are found in my community and they are disbelief: accusing in the genealogy and wailing."

He also said, "Whoever has intercourse with a woman from the rear he has disbelieved in what was revealed to Muhammad."

In another Hadith he said, "Anyone who goes to a fortune teller or soothsayer and believes in what he said is a disbeliever in what is revealed to Muhammad."

He also said, "After me, do not turn into unbelievers cutting the necks of one another."

This is the interpretation of Ibn Abbas and common Companions of the following verse: **"Those who do not judge according to what Allah has revealed are unbelievers."** *(5:44)*

Ibn Abbas said, "It is not disbelief that takes a man out of religion. It is not like disbelieving in Allah and the Last Day."

Tawus said, "It is disbelief below the disbelief, injustice below the injustice and disobedience below the disobedience."

Some scholars interpreted the verse as abandoning to judge according to what Allah has revealed by rejecting it. This statement is attributed to 'Ikrimah. This is an improbable interpretation. The very rejection of it is disbelief whether he judged or not.

Some others explained it as abandoning judgement by all that Allah has revealed. They say that it included the order of belief in the oneness of Allah and Islam. It is also far-fetched. The threat for not judging by what is revealed includes abandoning all or some of the orders.

Another meaning given by some is that it applies to judge against the text intentionally. Others said it is applicable to the people of the Book.

Some scholars consider disbelief that makes the person lose their religion. The correct view is that judgement by other rules than what Allah has revealed includes both minor and major disbelief in accordance with the condition of the judge. If he believes that judgment by what Allah has revealed is obligatory, yet he turns away from it in disobedience and knowing that is an offence then it is a minor disbelief. But if he thinks that it is not obligatory and he has choice in it while he knows that it is the rule of Allah then it is the major disbelief. However, if he did not know or made a mistake, he is treated as being wrong.

The point is that all categories are part of minor disbelief because they are against the gratefulness which means to act according to the order of Allah. The act is either gratefulness or disbelief or neither from this or that. Allah knows best.

Major disbelief is of five types: rejection, arrogance and denial after accepting, aversion, doubt and hypocrisy.

a. Rejection means to think that the Messengers are telling lies. This type is few amongst the unbelievers because Allah gave support to His messengers and provided them with evidence for their truthfulness, which was enough to establish their cases and remove any excuses. Allah Almighty said about Pharaoh and his people:
"They denied them, in their wickedness and their pride, even though their souls acknowledged them as true." *(27:14)*

He, the Most High, said to His Messenger, may Allah's blessing and peace be upon him:
"It is not you they disbelieve: the evildoers reject Allah's revelation." *(6:33)*

b. The disbelief of arrogance and denial is like the disbelief of the Devil. He did not reject the order of Allah nor did he refuse it. He met it with disdain and arrogance. To this category belongs the disbelief of the person who realises the truth of the Messenger and knew that he has brought the truth from Allah. He did not criticise him because of arrogance and disdain. This is common in the enemies of the Messengers. Allah tell us about Pharaoh and his people who said
"Are we to believe in two mortals like us? And their people are our servants?" *(23:47)*

Other communities said similar things;
"You are only men like us." *(14:10)*

"In arrogant cruelty the people of Thamud called (their messenger) a liar." *(91:11)*

It is also the disbelief of the Jews as Allah tells us:
"When there came to them something they knew, they disbelieved it." *(2:89)*

He also said about them:
"They know it as well as they know their sons." *(2:146)*

This was also as the disbelief of Abu Talib. He considered the Messenger as true and had no doubt about it, but he was overwhelmed by the prejudice and respect of his fathers' religion and refused to accept his message.

c. The disbelief of aversion means to turn the ear and the heart from the Messenger and not to accept his call nor reject it. A person having this attitude does not pay attention to what is said and does not support or oppose the Messenger. It is how one of the members of Abd Yalail said to the Prophet 嶺, "By Allah, I am saying to you that if you are true then you are more honourable in my eyes than to refute you; but if you are telling a lie then you are lower than to be talked to."

d. The disbelief of doubt is based on doubt. A person in this situation does not remain so for long unless he has decided to ignore the signs of the truth of the Messenger ﷺ. He then does not listen to him and does not heed his words. If he pays attention to it he will have no doubt because his signs of truth are brighter than the evidence of the sun for the day.

e. The disbelief of hypocrisy is to express belief by tongue and hide denial in the heart. This is the greatest hypocrisy.

Disbelief of denial is of two types: general and specific.

General is to deny what Allah has revealed and His messengers altogether. The specific one is to deny an obligatory act of Islam or refuse to accept the prohibitions of the religion or any of the attributes of Allah or any matter He had mentioned, intentionally or in preference of the statement of someone who has adopted that view for any specific reason.

However, if a person denies any of the above matters out of ignorance or because of an excuse, he is not going to be declared as an unbeliever. An example is the report about the man who denied the power of Allah over him and asked his family to burn his body and spread his ashes in the air. In spite of that Allah forgave him because of his ignorance. He did it according to his knowledge and did not deny the power of Allah on recreating him out of stubbornness or disbelief.

SHIRK OR ASCRIBING PARTNERS TO ALLAH (Polytheism)
Shirk, association of partners with Allah, is of two types: major and minor.

The major one is not forgiven without repentance. It means to take a rival to Allah and love him as Allah is loved. This is shirk, which implies putting the gods of the polytheists on the same level with Lord of the universe. The polytheist will say in Hell:
"We were clearly misguided when we made you equal with the Lord of the worlds."
(26:97-98)

They will say it despite their confession that Allah alone was the Creator, Provider and Owner of everything, and their gods were unable to create or give provision; they cannot give life or cause death. Most, or rather all, polytheists still loved them, gave them respect and worshipped them besides Allah. Some of them love, favour and glorify them more than Allah Almighty. They rejoice when they are mentioned more than they do with the mention of Allah and feel angry when their deities are condemned or criticised much more than they do when Allah the Lord of the universe is criticised. If their idols' sanctity is violated they feel furious but when Allah's honour is treated with disrespect they do not move. If the person who disparaged their idols feed them something, they are happy with him and do not feel angry with him. This has been witnessed by us and others. You will see one of them having the name of his idol consistently on his tongue, calling in every situation. He calls upon him when he is ill or feels lonely. In all such situations he remembers his idol instead of Allah, thinking that he will help him with Allah and plead for him.

This was the condition of the idol worshippers in the past, which was passed from generation to generation. The earlier polytheists took idols of stones, but others took mankind as their deity. Allah, the Most High tells us about the predecessors of these polytheists:
"Those who chose other protectors beside Him, saying, 'We only worship them because they bring us nearer to Allah. Allah Himself will judge between them regarding their difference." *(39:3)*

Then the Almighty asserted that they are lying and are unbelievers, and that He will not guide them:
"Allah does not guide any ungrateful liar." *(39:3)*

This is the condition of that who takes a supporter other than Allah, thinking that he will bring him nearer to Allah. How rare are those who are safe from it? But how rare are those who do not show enmity towards the one who criticises it?

These polytheists and their predecessors think that their gods will intercede to Allah for them. This is the essence of shirk, which Allah has rejected and refuted in His Book. He, glory be to Him, has affirmed that all intercession rests with Allah. No one is able to intercede to Him except the one to whom He gives permission and whose statements and acts are acceptable to Him. These are the people of pure Tawhid who have not taken anyone beside Allah as their intercessor. They are the luckiest people as Allah will allow them to intercede because they never turned to anyone for help and intercession.

Intercession which Allah and His Messenger ﷺ have affirmed is that which is done with the permission of Allah for someone who has firm belief in His oneness. Intercession that Allah has rejected is that which the polytheists believe in, who take other than Allah as their supporters. They will be treated the opposite to what they had believed in and it is only the sincere believers who will gain it.

Consider the answer of the Prophet ﷺ to Abu Hurayrah when he asked him, "Who will be lucky to enjoy your intercession, O messenger of Allah?" He ﷺ replied, "'The luckiest people to benefit from my intercession are those who said 'there is no god but Allah' sincerely from the bottom of their hearts."

The Messenger ﷺ made the sincere declaration of Tawhid the greatest source of receiving his intercession. The polytheists believe that their worship of their idols is going to make them gain their intercession.

A polytheist believes that those who he has taken as supporters and intercessors will help him with Allah, as is the case with close friends of kings. They help their companions. They do not realise that no one can plead with Allah without His permission and He will allow the intercession only for those people whose words and acts He has approved. He said:
"Who is there that can intercede with Him except by His leave?" *(2:255)*

"They cannot intercede for anyone without His approval." *(21:28)*

He does not approve any word or act except that which comes out of belief in the oneness of Allah and following the Messenger ﷺ. All the earlier and later people will be questioned about these two matters: 'What did you worship? How did you respond to the messengers?' There are these three basic things which cut the tree of the shirk from the heart of anyone who understands them: No intercession without the permission of Allah; His permission is only for those whose word and actions He approves, and He does not approve any word or action except the one which is based on belief in oneness of Allah and obedience to the Messenger.

Allah, the Most High is not going to forgive those who set equals to Him, as He said:
"Then the disbelievers set equal to their Lord." *(6:1)*

They turn to others in worship, love and friendship, as He cited their statement in the following verse:
"By Allah, we were clearly misguided when we made you equal with the Lord of the universe." *(26:97-98)*

The Almighty described their behaviour:
"There are some who choose to worship others besides Allah as rivals to Him loving them as is due to Allah." *(2:165)*

You will notice that the words and acts of the polytheists oppose his claim. He says that we do not love them as is due to Allah and we do not set them as equal to Him, but he shows his anger when their idols are criticised more than is due to Allah. He feels happy when they are mentioned, especially when such things are said which are not in their power - such as helping the depressed, removing someone's troubles or fulfilling their needs. You will notice that a polytheist expresses happiness and his heart throbs and the emotions of submission and obedience rise. When you mention Allah alone and express His oneness he feels anguish, distress and agony. He will accuse you of reducing the quality of being the Lord, and he may hate you.

We have seen them clearly and were accused of hating them. They tried to devise plans to cause us trouble. Allah will humiliate them in the world and in the Hereafter. The only excuse they had in all such activities, as their polytheist brothers had, was that these people had disgraced our gods. They claimed that our Shaykhs who are our gates to Allah were being dishonoured. This is what the Christians said to the Prophet ﷺ when he declared Jesus to be the servant of Allah. They said to him, "you have dishonoured and disgraced the Messiah." The like of the polytheists' answer was similar to those who tried to stop them from taking the graves as places of worship and going to the mosques for other reasons which Allah and His Messenger have allowed. They said, "You have disgraced the people buried there."

Look at the similarity in their hearts as though they have advised one another. Allah says about these people:
"Those whom Allah guides are rightly guided, but you will find no protector to lead to the right path He leaves to stray." *(18:17)*

Allah, glory be to Him, has cut off all the bonds the polytheists want to stick to. A man of knowledge and sense knows that anyone who takes a person other than Allah as a protector or intercessor is "Like a spider building itself a house- the spider's house is the frailest of all houses." *(29:41)*

Allah said:
"Say: call upon your so-called gods besides Allah: they do not control even the weight of a speck of dust in heaven or earth, nor do they have any share in them, nor are any of them of any help to Allah. Intercession will not work with Him, except by those to whom He gives permission." *(34:22-23)*

A polytheist takes an object as god, thinking that it will bring benefit to him. But benefit can come only from a person who has one of the following four qualities:

a. He possesses the material which the worshipper is asking for,
b. if he is not the owner then he is the partner of the owner,
c. if he is not the partner then he is his helper and supporter,
d. if he is not even that then he is an intercessor to him.

Allah, glory be to Him, denied any of the four levels moving from the top to the bottom. He denied the ownership, partnership, support and intercession which the polytheist thinks that his idol has got power to do. He established intercession in which a polytheist has no share and that is the one for which He gives permission.

The above verse should be sufficient as light, evidence to establish the pure Tawhid, and root out all the bases and materials of shirk for anyone who pays attention to it. The Qur'an is full of such illustrations and explanations, but the majority of the people do not realise that their actions are included in them. They think that these examples belong to people who have gone before without leaving behind any successor. This kind of thinking is the one which comes between the heart and understanding the Qur'an. Although those people have passed away but they were succeeded by people either like them or worse. The Qur'an deals with both groups. The matter is as Umar b. Al-Khattab said, "The bonds of Islam will be broken bit by bit when such people come up in Islam who do not know the pre-Islamic traditions."

If a person is not aware of pre-Islamic trends and the modes of shirk and the acts which the Qur'an has condemned and disapproved, he is going to fall in it and call others to follow him. He does not know that what he is following is the same as people before Islam practised, or it is worse than that. In this way the teachings of Islam will go away from his heart and a good matter will turn to bad and the bad to good, and the Sunnah to innovation and the innovation to Sunnah. The result will be that a man will be declared as disbeliever because he has pure faith in the oneness of Allah. He will be called an innovator because he follows the Messenger 鬒, and deserts his vain desires and innovations. A man with the quality of discernment and understanding sees it clearly. Allah's help is sought.

The minor shirk include slight showing off, pretension for the people and taking oaths by others than Allah. The Messenger of Allah 鬒 said, "Whoever takes an oath by anyone other than Allah, commits shirk."

It also includes such statements about others, such as, "What Allah willed and you." "This is from Allah and you." "I am by Allah and you." "I have no one except Allah and you." "I put my trust in Allah and you." "If you were not there this or that would not have happened." This type of statement could be a greater shirk, depending on the intention of the speaker. It is reported that the a man said, "What Allah willed and you." The Prophet 鬒 replied, "Did you make an equal to Allah? Say 'what Allah alone willed.'"

The above statement is lighter than the others.

One of the modes of shirk is prostration of the disciple to the Shaykh. It is shirk on the part of both the one who does it and the one for whom it is done. It is strange that they say that it is not prostration, but he is bowing his head before the Shaykh in respect and submission. It could be said to them that it is shirk no matter what you call it. The reality of prostration is to put the head before someone. In this way prostration is done before the idols, the sun, the stars, the stones. In all this, the head is bowed before something.

Another type is the bowing down of turbaned people to one another when they meet. This is how the words of Allah "Enter the gate bowing down" *(2:58)* is explained because it is not possible to enter by the forehead at the ground.

Another type is to shave the head for the Shaykh. It is devotion to other than Allah. This act is done only to express the devotion to Allah in pilgrimage.

One of the kinds of shirk is to repent to the Shaykh. This is the greater shirk. Repentance is only to Allah, as is prayer, fasting, pilgrimage and offering the sacrifice. All these are the rights of Allah. It related in the Musnad that a prisoner was brought to the Messenger of Allah ﷺ and he said, "O Allah, I return in repentance to You and not to Muhammad." The Messenger ﷺ said, "This man has recognised the right to the one to whom it belongs."

Repentance is a mode of worship which can be done to Allah alone, such as prostration and prayer.

Another example of shirk is to make a vow to someone other than Allah. It is more serious than taking an oath by someone other than Allah. According to a statement of the Messenger ﷺ, "If a person takes an oath by anyone other than Allah, he has committed shirk".

Then what will be the case of the man who makes vows to others? Uqbah b. Amir related that the Messenger of Allah ﷺ said, "Vowing is swearing."

Among the categories of shirk are to fear of someone other than Allah, to trust someone other than Allah, to work for someone other than Allah, to show humility, respect and submission to him, to seek provision from him and to praise him for what Allah has granted. It also includes expressing anger and displeasure on the decrees of Allah, and belief that things can take place in the world against what Allah wills.

Another kind of shirk is to turn to and implore dead people to fulfil the needs. This is the root of the shirk of the common people. A person's work comes to an end with his death. He cannot bring any benefit or harm to himself, let alone to the one who beseeches him to fulfil his needs. To ask him to intercede with Allah for him is an ignorance of the intercessor and the one to whom it is made. It is mentioned earlier that no one can intercede with Allah without His permission, which is only granted to those who have full Tawhid. This polytheist came with something which is not accepted to Allah.

A dead person is in need of someone who can ask Allah for forgiveness, mercy and favour for him. Our Prophet ﷺ has taught us that when we visit the graves of the Muslims we should ask Allah to show mercy on them and forgive them. These polytheists reversed the case and visited the dead ones to seek help from them and to ask them to fulfil their needs. Their graves have been made into idols which are worshipped, and to visit them is considered a pilgrimage. They stay there and shave their heads. Thus they have combined the association with the right deity and changing His religion. They consider the followers of the path of Tawhid their enemies and accuse them of showing disrespect to the dead people. In reality they are the ones who show disrespect to the Creator by associating partners with Him and by accusing the believers in His oneness and taking them as their enemies. They also damaged the honour of those whom they associate with Allah by claiming that they are pleased with what is done to them and they are the ones who ordered them to do it. These are the enemies of the Messengers and the people of Tawhid in every place and time. They have a good number of followers. Ibrahim ﷺ, the friend of Allah prayed to Allah:

"Preserve me and my offspring from idolatry. Lord, they (idols) have led many people astray." *(14:35-36)*

Only those people are saved from this major shirk who have singled out Allah for worship and disassociate themselves from the polytheists. They take Allah alone as their friend and worship Him alone. Their love, fear, hope, submission, trust, seeking help, and turning for support centre on Him alone. They turn to Him alone and follow His commands in order to seek His pleasure. When they ask, they only ask Allah; when they seek help, they seek only His help; when they work they work for Him alone. They live for Allah, with Allah and in the company of Allah.

Shirk has many types, known only to Allah. If we start discussing them all, it will be too much for this book. Maybe Allah will guide us to compose a book about its categories, the causes, the sources, the harm and how it could be avoided. When a servant gets rid of shirk and *ta'til* (denying all attributes of Allah) all other matters are easier. But if he was trapped by them then he will perish and I have no sympathy with those who choose the path of perishing.

HYPOCRISY

As for hypocrisy it is the incurable inner disease. A man may be full of it but does not realise. It is something which is hidden from the people and often the person afflicted with it is not aware of it. He feels that he is doing the right thing while he is spoiling it.

Hypocrisy is of two kinds: major and minor. The major one will lead its man to the lowest depth of Hell. It is to show the Muslims that he believes in Allah, His angels, His books, His Messengers and the Hereafter, while in his heart he denies them. He does not believe that Allah spoke to a human being and revealed His words to him to guide people and to warn them of His punishment and give good tidings to them.

Allah, the Exalted, has exposed the hypocrites and revealed their secrets in the Qur'an. He brought their behaviour to light for His servants to make them aware of them and their tricks. He mentioned three groups: the believers, the disbelievers and the hypocrites in the beginning of the Chapter two. He mentioned the believers in four verses, disbelievers in two and the hypocrites in thirteen. He did this because of the large number of them and their danger to Islam and its followers. Islam's trial with these people is very serious because they claim to be Muslim and to help it, while in reality they are its enemies. They bring out their enmity in a form which an ignorant person thinks to be based on knowledge and understanding, but it is the utmost ignorance and corruption.

How many fortresses of Islam have they ruined? How many strongholds of it have they demolished? How many signs have they erased? How many raised banners have they brought down? How many doubts have they planted in the roots of its basic principles in order to confuse people? How many pure sources of its teachings have they polluted by their wrong opinions in order to damage them?

Islam and its followers continue suffering from their schemes and face doubt after doubt to confuse the matter. They claim to improve its teachings but they are spoiling them.
"They are causing corruption though they do not realise." *(2:12)*

"They wish to put Allah's light out with their mouths, but Allah will complete His light, even though the disbelievers hate it." *(61:8)*

They have come together to abandon the revelation and agreed not to be guided by it.

"They divided their religion among them into sects, each rejoicing in their own." *(23:53)*

"They suggest alluring words to one another in order to deceive." *(6:112)*

For that reason,
"They have taken this Qur'an as something to be abandoned." *(25:30)*

The signposts of the belief have been erased from their hearts, so they do not recognise them. Its centres have been extinct and they are not trying to reinstate them. Its bright stars have left from their hearts and they do not bring them to life. Its sun has been eclipsed in the darkness of their opinions and they are unable to see it. They did not accept the guidance which Allah sent with His messengers. They paid no attention to it and did not see anything wrong in abandoning it in favour of their opinions and thoughts. They stripped off the texts of the revelation from the power of reality and removed them from the position of certainty. They launched on them the raids of false interpretations. Every now and then they are ambushed by them. These Divine texts came to them like a guest who visited mean people, and was met by unworthy behaviour. They received him from far away and turned their hearts from him saying, "You are not allowed to stay with us, except to pass by." They prepared numerous rules and regulations to repel him. They said when they were faced by them, "What can we do with the apparent meanings which cannot lead us to certainty." Their common people said, "Sufficient for us is that upon which we found our later scholars. They are more knowledgeable than earlier scholars about the correct evidences and arguments."

These are the people who are simple with clear hearts. They are unable to understand the method of looking into the principles of religion. They turned their efforts towards doing what is commanded and abandoning what is prohibited. The method of the later scholars is based on knowledge and is solid while the method of the earlier ones is simple but safe.

They awarded the texts of the Qur'an and the Sunnah the position of the caliph of the time. His name is on the coins and read in the sermons on the pulpits, but the orders of others are carried out. The dictates of the Divine sources are not followed or accepted.

They have put on the dress of the people of faith while inside their hearts they hide the germs of cheating, disbelieving and misguidance. From outside they appear like the helpers but inside they are the disbelievers. Their tongues are those of peace lovers but their hearts are those of warriors. They claim that they believe in Allah and the Last Day while in fact they are not believers.

Their capital is stratagem and treachery, and their commodity is lies and deception. They think that both groups are pleased with them and they are safe among them.

"They deceive Allah and those who believe, but they deceive none but themselves and do not perceive." *(2:9)*

The diseases of doubts and desires have worn out their hearts and destroyed them. The bad wishes dominated their intentions and purposes and spoiled them. Their corruption has led them to the destruction to the extent that the expert doctors failed to treat them.
"There is a disease in their hearts, which Allah has added to. Agonizing torments awaits them for their persistent lying." *(2:10)*

When the claws of their doubts catch on the skin of their faith, they tore it completely. When the flame of their sedition touches the heart of anybody, it puts it in the torment of the Fire. When the suspicions of their deceit enter the ears of someone they make a barrier between his heart and accepting the belief. Their sedition on earth is great but many people are unaware of it.

"When it is said to them, 'Do not cause corruption in the land', they say, 'We are only putting things right', but really they are causing corruption, thought they do not realise it." *(2:11-12)*

A man who adheres to the Book and the Sunnah is considered a man of literal meaning by them. They regard him as having very little share of reasoning. Such people who revolve around the texts regarded by them as donkeys carrying books. Their concern is only with learning the tradition and the study of the revelation, which is not acceptable to them. Those who follow the religious teachings are considered foolish by them, they consider them an evil omen in their meetings.

"When it is said to them, 'Believe, as other people believe,' they say 'Should we believe as fools do?' but they are fools, though they do not know it." *(2:13)*

Every one of them has two faces - one for the believers and the other to show their heretical colleagues. They have two tongues, one they use when they meet the Muslims and the other which expresses their secrets.

"When they meet the believers, they say, 'We believe', but when they are alone with their evil ones, they say, 'Indeed we are with you; we were only mocking.'" *(2:14)*

They turned away from the Book and the Sunnah to express their disdain and mockery to their followers. They refused to accept the rulings of the two revelations, being happy with the knowledge they have in arrogance and pride. They always mock at those who follow the clear revelation.

"Allah mocks them, and allows them in their transgression to wander blindly." *(2:15)*

They set out in search of unprofitable trade in the seas of darkness, and embarked on the boats of doubts and suspicions which sail in the waves of imaginations. Their boats are thrashed by the storm wind and destroyed.

"They are the ones who bought error in exchange for guidance, so their trade reaps no profit, and they are not rightly guided." *(2:16)*

The fire of belief provided them with light and they saw the positions of guidance and error, then that light went away and there remained only a raging fire. They are punished by that fire and blindly wander in the darkness.

"Their example is that of one who kindled a fire, but when it illuminated what was around them, Allah took away their light and left them in darkness, so they could not see." *(2:17)*

The ears of their hearts are covered with heaviness, so they are unable to listen to the caller of belief. Their eyes are covered and they are unable to see the realities of the Qur'an. Their tongues are dumb for the truth and they are unable to speak of it.

"They are deaf, dumb and blind: they will never return." *(2:18)*

The rain of the revelation came to them, which had the life of the hearts and the souls, but they could hear only the thunder of threat, warning and the duties which were assigned to them in the morning and evening. They put their fingers in their ears and covered themselves with their dress and hurried away. The chase after them was earnest, and they were spotted and called out in public and their real condition was exposed to all those who could see. The examples of both their groups, the ones who argued and those who were imitators, were cited and it was said:

"Or it is like a rainstorm from the sky within which is darkness, thunder and lightening. They put their fingers in their ears against the thunderclaps for fear of death. Allah surrounds the disbelievers." *(2:19)*

The vision of their insight was unable to stand the lightening of the brightness of the message and the radiance of its meanings. Their ears failed to receive the thunders of its threats and its obligations and prohibitions. They stood puzzled before it in the valley of wilderness where no sound is heard and nothing can be seen.

"Whenever it flashes on them they walk on and when darkness falls around them they stand still. If Allah so willed, He could take away their hearing and sight. Allah has power over everything." *(2:20)*

There are indications mentioned in the Qur'an and the Sunnah by which they can be recognised by anyone who has been gifted with the insight of the faith. They stood up with show off, which is the worst thing to do. They felt lazy to carry out the orders of the Most Merciful. Sincerity has become a burden to them and the result is in the following:
"When they stand up to pray, they do so sluggishly, showing off in front of people, and remember Allah only a little." *(4:142)*

One of them is like a goat straying between two sheep, who drifts between one and the other but does not settle with either of them. They stand between two groups deciding which one is stronger and more powerful.

"Wavering all the time between this and that, belonging neither to one side nor the other. When Allah leaves someone astray, you will never find a way for him." *(4:143)*

They wait for fortune to turn against the people of the Qur'an and the Sunnah. If there is victory for them, they say; 'Were we not on your side?' They swear by Allah with their most solemn oaths. But if the balance is in the favour of the enemies of the Book and the Sunnah, they say, "Do you not realise that the pledge of brotherhood is strong between us, and we are close to one another?" Anyone who is interested in knowing about them let him learn about their characters from the words of the Lord of the universe:

"They wait to see what happens to you, and if Allah brings you success, they say to them, 'Were we not on your side?' but if the disbelievers have some success, they say to them, Did we not have the upper hand over you, and protect you from the believers? Allah will judge between you all on the Day of Resurrection and He will give the disbelievers no means of overcoming the believers." *(4:141)*

The sweet and soft talk of one of them is admired by the listeners. He calls on Allah to witness what is in his heart, despite his lies and falsehood. You will see him sleeping on the truth but active with falsehood. Take their description from the statement of the Holy and the Source of peace:

"And of the people is he whose speech pleases you in worldly life, and he even calls Allah to witness what is in his heart, yet he is the fiercest of opponents." *(2:204)*

The instructions they give to their followers contain destruction of the towns and the people. They prohibit them from what is good for their affairs in this life and the Hereafter. You meet one of them amongst the group of the believers in prayer, remembrance, hard work and indifference to the worldly matters.

"When he goes away, he strives to spread corruption throughout the land destroying crops and livestock. Allah does not like corruption." *(2:205)*

They belong to the same category, resembling one another. They enjoin what is wrong after they have done it and forbid what is right after neglecting it. They do not spend their wealth in the way of Allah and to seek His pleasure. Allah reminded them very often of His favours, yet they turned away from His remembrance and forget Him. He exposed their secrets to His believing servants in order to avoid them. Listen to what He says:

"The hypocrites, both men and women, are all the same: they order what is wrong and forbid what is right; they are tight-fisted. They have forgotten Allah, so He has forgotten them. The hypocrites are the disobedient ones." *(9:67)*

If you try to take them to the clear dictates of the revelation for judgement, you will find them showing distaste, and if you invite them to the decision of the Book of Allah and the Sunnah of His Messenger 🏵 you will see them turning away. If you know their realities you will see a long distance between them and guidance, and you will notice that they are extremely averse to the revelation.

"When it is said to them: 'Come to what Allah has revealed and to the Messenger, you see the hypocrites turn away from you completely." *(4:61)*

How then they can they achieve success and guidance after their reasoning and beliefs are affected? How can they get rid of the misguidance and destruction when they have purchased disbelief in exchange of belief? How unprofitable is their trade when they have exchanged fire for sealed nectar?

"How will it be if disaster strikes them because of what they themselves have done, and they come to you, swearing by Allah, "We only wanted to do good and achieve harmony."

The bitter tree of *Zaqqum* of doubts and suspicions has stuck in their hearts and they do not find a way to swallow it.

"Those are the ones of whom Allah knows what is in their hearts, so turn away from them but admonish them and speak to them a far-reaching word." *(4:63)*

May they perish! How far away they are from the reality of belief! Their claim of investigation and knowledge is completely false. They have their concern and the believers have their own concern. Allah, the Most High, swore in His Book by His own Holy Being, the people of discernment understand its content because their hearts are full of honour and respect for Him. He said warning His servants and telling the real position of these people:

"By your Lord, they will not be true believers until they let you decide between them in all matters of dispute, and find no resistance in their souls to your decisions, accepting them totally." *(4:65)*

One of them swears before he speaks without being questioned because he knows that the hearts of the people of belief do not feel reassured to his word. He, therefore, wants to save himself from poor opinions about him and being exposed. This is how the people of doubt tell lies and swear to convince the listener that they are telling the truth.

"They use their oath as a cover and so bar others from Allah's way. Indeed it was evil what they were doing." *(63:2)*

May they perish! They came out to the desert with the troops of the faith, but they saw the long way and distant journey and they turned back on their heels and returned. They thought they would enjoy a pleasant life and sweet sleep in their homes, but it did not work and they did not enjoy the sleep. Before long a crier cried out and they left their dinner tables without being satisfied. What will be their condition at the time of meeting with Allah? They knew then that they rejected, saw the truth then closed their eyes.

"They professed faith and then rejected it, so their hearts have been sealed and they do not understand." *(63:3)*

They have good bodies, fascinating tongues, charming discourse, but vicious hearts and weak souls. They are like pieces of wood propped up which have no fruit. They have been pulled up from their roots and reclined against a wall to stand so that they are not crushed by the passers by.

"When you see them, their forms please you, and when they speak you listen to what they say. But they are like the propped-up timbers - they think every cry they hear is against them - and they are the enemy. Beware of them. May Allah destroy them! How are they deluded?" *(63:4)*

They delay the prayer from its beginning of the time to the last moment and perform the dawn prayer at the time of sunrise and the afternoon one at the sunset. They peck up like the crow. Their prayer is the prayer of bodies not of the hearts. They turn around during it like a fox which feels that it is being chased for hunting. They do not attend the congregation and perform the prayers inside their homes or shops. When they argue they use obscene language. When they enter a pledge they betray, when they speak they tell lies, when they make promises they do not fulfil them and when they are given trust they betray it. This is how they behave with the Creator and the creation. Learn about their characters from the beginning of the chapter of "Those who give short measure" *(83)* and the last part of "The night-comer" *(86)*. None can inform you about their characters like the One who is aware of everything.

"Prophet, strive hard against the disbelievers and the hypocrites, and be tough with them. Hell is their final home - an evil destination!" *(9:73, 66:9)*

How many are they? In reality they are few. But how powerful they look while they are weak. How ignorant they are, yet they try to appear as learned. How deceived are they about Allah as they are unaware of His greatness.

"They swear by Allah that they belong to you, but they do not. They are cowardly." *(9:56)*

If the people of the Book and the Sunnah meet with victory and upper hand, it causes them worry and concern, but if trials from Allah comes to them in order to test them and to wipe out their sins, they feel happy and rejoice.

"If you have good fortune, it will grieve them, but if misfortune comes your way, they will say to themselves, 'We took precaution for this,' and go away rejoicing. Say, 'Only what Allah has decreed will happen to us. He is our Master: let the believers put their trust in Allah." *(9:50-51)*

Allah Almighty also said about those who remained behind at the battle of Uhud:
"They grieve at any good that befalls you and rejoice at your misfortunes. But if you are steadfast and conscious of Allah, their scheming will not harm you in the least. Allah encircles everything they do." *(3:120)*

Allah disliked their good deeds because of the wickedness of their hearts and the corruption of their intentions. He made them stay behind. The Almighty disliked their approach to Him because they were inclined to His enemies, so He drove them away and banished them. They turned away from His revelation, so He turned away from them. He caused them to suffer and did not grant them happiness. He passed a fair judgement about them after which there remained no hope for their success unless they become among the repentant. He said:
"If they had really wanted to go out (to battle) with you, they would have made preparations, but Allah was loath to let them rise up and made them hold back. It was said, 'Stay with those who stay behind." *(9:46)*

He then mentioned the wisdom for making them stay behind and driving them from His door, and that was His kindness and help for His friends. He said, and He is the best of the judges:
"Had they gone forth they would not have increased you except in confusion, and they would have been active among you seeking to cause dissension. And some of you would willingly have listened to them. Allah knows exactly who does evil." *(9:47)*

The Divine texts were heavy to them so they disliked them. They found them beyond their power so they dropped them from their shoulders. The Prophetic Traditions were too difficult for them to remember so they ignored them. The texts of the Book and the Sunnah assaulted them, and to dismiss them they invented rules and regulations. Allah has revealed their secrets and uncovered their schemes, and set their examples for His servants. He told them that whenever a group of them becomes extinct others take their place. Almighty described them by their characters to warn His servants and make them aware of them. He said:
"It is because they hate what Allah has sent down that He caused their deeds to go waste." *(47:9)*

This is the condition of a person who finds the texts burdensome and sees them as barrier between himself and his innovations and desires. They appear to him like a structure joined firmly. He sold them only for the theory of false words. He exchanged them with *Fusus* and this spoiled for him his open and secret actions.

"They say to those who hate what Allah has sent down, 'We will obey you to some matters' - Allah knows their secret schemes. How will they feel when the angels take them in death, beating their faces and their backs because they practised things that incurred Allah's wrath and disdained to please Him? So He made their deeds go to waste." *(47:26-28)*

They tried to hide the secrets of hypocrisy but Allah disclosed them on their faces and in their talks. The Almighty stamped them with marks which are not hidden on the people of discretion and the faith. They thought that by hiding their disbelief and expressing their faith they have succeeded to deceive the people of discernment and judgement. They did not realise that the Great Judge has exposed them.

"Do the corrupt at heart assume that Allah will not expose their malice? We could even point them out to you (Prophet) if we wished, and then you could identify them by their marks, but you will know them anyway by the tone of their speech. Allah knows everything you do." *(47:29-30)*

What will they fare when they are gathered on the day of assembly, and Allah will appear before His servants and the sins will be disclosed? They will be invited to prostrate but they will not be able to do so.

"Their eyes will be downcast and they will be overwhelmed with shame. They were invited to prostrate themselves when they were safe." *(68:43)*

Or how will it be when they will be dragged to the bridge of Hell? It is thinner than a hair and sharper than a sword. It will be very slippery and dark. Nobody will be able to cross it except with a light which will make him see his footsteps. Lights will be distributed among the people according to their faith. The people will cross at different speeds. These hypocrites will also be given a light with the people of faith, as they were with them openly fulfilling the duties of prayer, zakat, and pilgrimage and fasting. When they reach the middle of the bridge the winds of hypocrisy will carry away their lights and they will stand confused, unable to go ahead. At that moment a door will be erected between them and the people of faith - to the side of the believers will be mercy, and their side will have torment and revenge. They will call the people of faith, who are ahead of them and whose lights will appear from the distance, like stars:
"Wait for us! Let us have some of your light!" *(57:13)*

They will call and say, "Our light has gone out, so help us to cross this narrow pass. We are not able to cross it without light." The answer will be, "Go back and look for a light." *(57:14)*

How difficult is it for anyone to stand in such a race track? They will ask, "How can we stop in this narrow pass? Can anyone turn to another in it? Can a friend help his friend in this situation?" They will try to remind the believers of their companionship in this world as a stranger reminds a native of their companionship in journey. They will ask, "Were we not with you? We fasted as you did, performed prayers as you did, read the Qur'an like you, gave charity and performed hajj. Why then there is a difference between you and us? You alone crossed the pass and we were left." The believers will reply, "Yes, but your outside was with us and your inside was with the disbelievers and every ungrateful unjust man."

"But you allowed yourselves to be tempted, you were hesitant, doubtful, deceived by false hopes until Allah's command came. The Deceiver tricked you about Allah. Today no ransom will be accepted from you or from the disbelievers; your home is the Fire - that is where you belong - a miserable destination." *(57:14-15)*

Do not ponder too much over what has been said. As a matter of fact what has been left out is more than what has been said. All parts of the Qur'an seem to be about them because of their large number on the earth and inside the graves. May the places of the earth not be empty from their presence so that the believers do not feel insecure in their ways! If this happens the sources of life will be abandoned and the people of faith will be grabbed by the beasts and wild animals in the deserts. Hudhayfah ♦ heard a man saying, "O Allah, destroy the hypocrites!" He said to him, "Son of my brother, if the hypocrites are destroyed you will feel insecure in your streets due to the lack of walking people."

Fear of hypocrisy cut the hearts of the early people into pieces because they were aware of its small and great details completely. They developed poor opinions of themselves and feared that they may be among the hypocrites. Umar b. Al-Khattab ♦ said to Hudhayfah, "I implore you by Allah, tell me whether the Messenger of Allah, may Allah's blessing and peace be upon him, counted me among them." Hudhayfah replied, "No, but I will not vindicate anyone after you."

Ibn Abu Mulaykah said, "I met thirty of the Companions of the Prophet Muhammad, may Allah's blessing and peace be upon him, and each one of them was scared of hypocrisy about himself. None of them said his belief was like the belief of Gabriel and Michael." This has been cited by Bukhari.

Hasan al-Basari is reported to have said, "None but a hypocrite feels secure from Allah, and none but a believer has fear of Him."

It is also reported that one of the Companions used to pray, "O Allah I seek refuge in You from the humility of hypocrisy." He was asked what the humility of hypocrisy was. He replied, "To have the sign of humbleness on your body while your heart has no such thing in it."

By Allah, their hearts were filled with faith and certainty and they were very much scared of hypocrisy. They were always preoccupied with its danger. But now there are many people whose belief does not go beyond their throats, yet they claim that their belief is like the belief of Gabriel and Michael.

The plant of the hypocrisy grows on two stalks - lying and showing off - and is irrigated by the lack of discernment and will. When all these elements are found, the plant of hypocrisy becomes stronger and more solid. However, it is similar to a flood on the brink of a crumbling precipice. When they witness the torrent of the realities on the Day when the secrets are laid bare and hidden matters are disclosed, the contents of the graves are scattered and the secrets of the hearts are uncovered, those whose commodity was hypocrisy will realise that their deeds were like a mirage.

"The deeds of the disbelievers are like a mirage in a desert, the thirsty person thinks there will be water, when he gets there, he finds it is nothing. There he finds only Allah. Who pays him his account in full. Allah is swift in reckoning." *(24:39)*

Their hearts are heedless of the good deeds while their bodies run to the luxury of the world. Immorality is rampant in their compartments. When they hear the truth their hearts are hard, and when they come to the falsehood and lies the eyes of their hearts are open, and their ears listen to what is said.

These are the signs of hypocrisy. So take care, O man, before judgement is passed on you. The hypocrites do not fulfil their pledge when they make one, they break their promises, they speak untruthfully, and when they are invited to the obedience, they hesitate. When it is said to them, "Come to what Allah has sent down and to the Messenger," they turn away, but when their desires and lust invite them, they hurry and rush to them. Leave them with the humiliation they have chosen for themselves, and let them face disgrace and loss. Do not trust their promises and do not believe in their words. They are liars, and bent on betraying you.

"There are some among them who pledged themselves to Allah, saying, 'If Allah gives us some of His bounty, we will certainly give alms and be righteous,' yet when He gave them some of His bounty, they became mean and turned obstinately away. Because they broke their promise to Allah, because of all the lies they told, He made hypocrisy settle in their hearts until the Day they meet Him." *(9:75-77)*

DEFIANCE

Regarding defiance, it is of two kinds in the Book of Allah: Single and mixed with disobedience. The single one is also of two types: defiance that leads to disbelief and that which does not take a man out of Islam.

The defiance which is mixed is mentioned in the following statement of Allah, the Great:
"Allah has endeared faith to you and made it beautiful to your hearts; He made disbelief, defiance and disobedience hateful to you. Those are the rightly guided." *(49:7)*

The single one which is disbelief is cited in the following verses:
"Through it He makes many go astray and leads many to the right path. But it is only the defiant He makes go astray, those who break their covenant with Allah after it has been confirmed, who sever the bonds that Allah has commanded to be joined and spread corruption on the earth." *(2: 26-27)*

"Indeed We have sent down clear messages to you and only those who defy would refuse to believe them." *(2: 99)*

"As for those who defy (Allah), their home will be the Fire. Whenever they try to escape it, they will be driven back into it, and they will be told, 'Taste the torment of the Fire, which you persistently denied." *(32: 20)*

All this is the defiance of disbelief. The defiance which does not cause a man to go out of Islam is mentioned in the following verses:
"If you do so, it is indeed defiance on your part." *(2: 282)*

"O you who believe, if a disobedient one comes to you with information, investigate it, lest you harm a people out of ignorance and become, over what you have done, regretful." *(49:6)*

This verse was revealed concerning al-Walid b. 'Uqbah b. Abu Mu'ayt , when the Messenger of Allah 🌸 sent him to Banu al-Mustaliq to collect charity. There was animosity between him and the tribe. When the people heard of him coming they came to receive him to show respect to the order of the Messenger of Allah 🌸. But Satan put it in his mind that they were coming to kill him. Feeling scared, he returned from the way to the Messenger of Allah 🌸 and said that Banu al-Mustaliq have refused to pay their dues of charity, and wanted to kill him. The Messenger of Allah 🌸 was enraged and intended to attack them.

When the tribe learned that the envoy of the Messenger 🌸 had gone back, they went to him and said, "Messenger of Allah, we heard of your envoy coming to us and we came out to receive and honour him. We wanted to pay the dues of Allah on us. But the man went back. We feared that his action may have been a message from you because you were angry with us for some reason. We seek the protection of Allah from His anger and His Messenger's anger."

The Messenger of Allah ﷺ became suspicious of them and sent Khaild b. Al-Walid with a contingent and ordered him to keep his arrival a secret. He told him to look for the signs of their faith, and collect the dues of their wealth, but if he could not see the signs of faith in them then he should treat them like disbelievers. Khalid followed the instructions of the Prophet ﷺ. When he reached their area, he heard the call for the prayers of Maghrib and 'Isha'. He took their dues and returned and told the Messenger of Allah ﷺ about their loyalty. Then the above verse was sent down.

There is an elegant point here. Allah, glory be to Him, did not order to reject the information of the defiant man and declare him a liar and so refuse all his testimony. He asked to investigate and to verify. If his truthfulness was confirmed by external evidence, his statement would have been accepted. This is how the report and testimony of a defiant person should be treated. Many defiant people tell the truth in their information and testimony, and many strive extremely to find the truth. This type of person's information and testimony are not to be rejected. If this is done, many rights would be impeded and true information would be rejected, especially when they come from the people of corrupt belief who are trying to tell the truth.

As for those who are liars, if they are known to tell lies constantly and without any reservation, so much so that their lies dominate their truth, their information and testimony are to be rejected. However, if he is known to tell lies only once or twice then according to some scholars his report and testimony will be accepted, although in others' opinions it will not be accepted.

Here we are concerned with the defiance which does not take a man out of Islam. The defiance from which repentance is required is wider than the defiance which makes a person to be rejected when he reports.

Our discussion here is about the actions from which repentance is required. And they are of two types: defiance in carrying out duties, and defiance concerning belief. Defiance in actions is also of two types: single or mixed with disobedience. The second one is to commit the things which Allah has forbidden. It means to disobey the commands of Allah as He said:
"They do not disobey Allah in what He commands them." *(66:6)*

And as Moses said to his brother Aaron:
"Aaron, what prevented you, when you realised that they had gone astray, from following me? Did you disobey my order?" *(20: 92-93)*

A poet says, "I gave you a definite order but you disobeyed me, and as a result I found myself out of power and regretful."

The word 'Fisq' is used especially for committing what is forbidden. Allah said:
"If you do so, it is defiance on your part." *(2:282)*

The word 'Ma'siyyah' on the other hand is used in violating the commanded matters. However, both are used interchangeably. Allah said:
"Except Iblis, he was one of the Jinn and he disobeyed the order of his Lord."

Here the disobedience of the Devil of the command is called *fisq* while in another place the violation of the prohibition of Allah is called *ma'siyyah* as it is in the following verse:
"Adam disobeyed his Lord and erred." *(20:121)*

This is when they are used alone, but when they are joined then one indicates the disobedience of the order and the other the violation of the prohibition.

The word 'taqwa' denotes avoiding both matters. By adopting it, repentance from defiance and disobedience will be correct. It means to work with the obedience of Allah by the light of Allah and hope for the reward of Allah; and to abandon the disobedience of Allah by the light of Allah, fearing His punishment.

The defiance of belief is found in the people of innovations who believe in Allah, His Messenger and the Hereafter. They consider what Allah has prohibited unlawful and take what He has declared as obligatory to be binding. But they deny many matters which Allah and His Messenger have affirmed, and claim things which Allah and His Messenger have not approved - all this out of ignorance and blind imitation of their peers. They are like *Khawarij, Rawafid, Mu'tazilah* and *Jahmiyya*. However, our intention is not to discuss their positions, but rather we are to deal with the repentance of the ten categories we listed above.

Repentance from this defiance is by accepting what Allah and His Messenger have affirmed about Allah, the Glorious without resorting to illustration and imagination. It also includes declaring Him above what He and His Messenger have declared without trying to interpret in a distorted way or denying attributes to Him. All the positive and negative aspects regarding the Almighty must be taken from the source of revelation, not from the opinions of the people and their thoughts, which are the source of innovation and misguidance.

The repentance of these defiant people who have corrupt beliefs revolve around the following of the Sunnah. That is not enough; they must explain the falsehood of the innovation they were involved in. Repentance from a crime depends on doing its opposite. This is borne by the fact that Allah made declaration a condition for the repentance of those who hid the guidance and evidence which Allah had revealed. Their sin was to hide, so their repentance is to declare. Allah, the Most High, said:

"As for those who hide the proofs and guidance We send down, after We have made them clear to people in the Book, Allah curses them, and so do others, unless they repent, make amends, and declare the truth. I will certainly accept their repentance: I am the Ever Relenting, the Most Merciful." *(2:159-160)*

The crime of the innovator is above the crime of the one who hides because he concealed the truth, but the former concealed it and called to its opposite.

The repentance of the hypocrite is to become sincere because his offence was showing off. Allah says about them:

"The hypocrites will be in the lowest depth of the Fire - and never will you find them a helper - except for those who repent, correct their ways, hold fast to Allah and become sincere in their religion for Allah. These will be joined with the believers. Allah is going to give the believers great reward." *(4:159-160)*

For this reason the correct opinion is that the repentance of an accuser is to declare that he has told lies. It is opposite of the sin he committed by disgracing an innocent Muslim. His repentance is to declare himself a liar so that the shame he caused the accused by his act can be removed. This is the objective of repentance.

The other opinion in this regard is that his repentance is to say, 'I seek forgiveness from Allah from accusation'. This is a weak view as there is no benefit for the accused and he is not going to regain his honour. Hence, the objective of the repentance from this sin is not achieved. It is to be noted that the crime of accusation has two rights: one for Allah, who has prohibited it. Repentance from it is by seeking forgiveness from Allah, acknowledging the prohibition of accusation, feeling regret over it and making a firm intention to not repeat it. The second is the right of the servant to whom he caused shame, and its repentance is only by the declaring of the accuser that he told a lie. Repentance of this crime is by both acts.

There is a question here: How can a man who has seen the act of adultery by his own eyes and spoke about it declare himself as a liar to fulfil the requirement of the repentance?

This is exactly what led the people say that his repentance is to acknowledge the prohibition of the accusation and seek forgiveness for it. It requires an explanation of the lie which Allah said the accuser committed. The Almighty said that he is a liar to Him even though his information is true.

Know that lying involves two matters: news that is not true - and this could be either deliberate or by mistake. A deliberate lie is known. An example of a lie by mistake is the false statement of Abu al-Sanabil b. Bakack, regarding the woman whose husband passed away and she delivered a child. He said that she will not be free until four month and ten days pass. The Messenger of Allah ﷺ said, "Abu al-Sanabil told a lie."

Another example is the statement of the Messenger ﷺ, "Whoever said it is a liar."

He said it about a person who had said, "The deeds of 'Amir were annulled because he killed himself."

Another example is the statement of 'Ubadah b. al-Samit when he said, "Abu Muhammad is telling lies," when he said that the witr prayer is obligatory. All these are examples of mistaken lies. The meaning is that the person who said it was wrong.

The second type of lie is information which is not allowed to pass. It may be true, such as the information of a person who witnessed alone the act of adultery and then accused the person. This person is a liar in the judgement of Allah, although his information is true. Allah said: **"If they did not produce the (required) witnesses, they are the liars in the eyes of Allah."** *(24: 13)*

Allah's ruling in such cases is that the person should be given the punishment of the liar, even though his information is correct. As such his repentance will not be complete unless he admits that he is a liar in the eyes of Allah. When Allah has declared him a liar and he does not admit this, what kind of repentance is for him? This is mere insistence and an open violation of the ruling of Allah Almighty.

There is a disagreement among the scholars in the case of the repentance of a thief whose hand has been cut. Is he required to return the stolen property to its owner?

They all agree that his repentance will be correct if he returns the stolen property, provided it is in his possession. But what will happen if it was consumed. There is no agreement among them. Al-Shafi'i and Ahmad say that his repentance will only be complete if he accepts the liability of the goods, and it is his responsibility whether he is poor or rich. Abu Hanifah on the other hand said that the correctness of his repentance did not depend on accepting the liability. Cutting off the hand is the full punishment. To make him responsible to return what was stolen is an addition to it, which is not right.

It is different from the situation where the stolen property is available. In this case the thief will have to return it and it is not an additional punishment. But if the property is consumed then to ask him to pay for it is an additional penalty, and it is wrong to impose on him the penalty of losing a part of his body and giving money. They argued that for this reason Allah did not mention in the punishment of the thief and that who wages war, an additional punishment other than carrying out the prescribed punishment.

The jurists of Madinah i.e. Malik and others, took a middle course and said that if he had money, he would have to compensate after the cutting off of his hand, but if he had no money then it was not necessary. This is a good opinion close to what the Shari'ah accepts. And Allah, the Most High, knows best.

TRANSGRESSION AND SINS

These are both connected. Allah, the Glorious, said:
"Help one another to do what is right and good; do not help one another towards sin and aggression." *(5:2)*

Each of them when cited alone includes the other. So, every sin is aggression as it involves doing what Allah has forbidden, or abandoning what He has commanded. This is aggression against His command and prohibition, and every aggression is a sin. However, when they are cited jointly then they mean different matters in accordance with their quality.

Sin is what is forbidden in itself, such as telling lies, committing adultery, drinking wine and so on. Aggression is connected with quantity and trespassing. It means to take more than is allowed, such as taking from a person more than is due. It could be taking more money than is due or hurting him in his body or honour. For example if a person has taken a piece of wood from someone and he tries to take his house in return, as compensation. Or if one person has caused damage to another's property, and the second person tries to damage more than what was done by the first. If one has spoken some bad words about another, the other wants to say more about the first. All these are forms of transgression and offence against justice.

This transgression is of two kinds: One is connected with the rights of Allah and the other deals with the rights of the servants. The case of transgression regarding the rights of Allah is like going beyond what Allah has allowed for a man. For instance Allah has allowed him to have intercourse with his wife or slave girl, but he goes beyond it to commit illicit acts with other women. Allah, the Most High, said about the believers:
"Who guard their chastity except with their spouses or their slaves - with these they are not to blame, but those who seek to go beyond this are exceeding the limits." *(23:5-7)*

It also includes exceeding what has been allowed from his wife and slave to what is forbidden, for instance, to have intercourse with them during their monthly period or use the back side or have sex whilst any of them are in ihram, or during his obligatory fast and so on.

Transgression also applies to a person who was allowed a limited amount of something and he went beyond that. The example is of a man who was allowed to swallow a sip of wine to prevent choking, but he drank the whole cup. Or a man who was given the permission to look at his fiancé, or a doctor checking a patient, who then took advantage and looked at more than what was allowed. He used this permission to gaze at the beautiful parts of the woman. By doing this he transgressed the permitted area to the forbidden one and entered in the protected sanctuary. Letting himself look affected his heart and produced serious consequences. This is what exceeding the limits can lead to.

He lost the enormous reward of lowering his gaze for the sake of Allah, the Great. He let his eyes roam and look at the attractiveness of his victim, yet got nothing in return. He deceived himself, without realising that this risk may cause him great danger. This was like a journey in the desert which led him away from what he intended. He did not complete his journey and was attacked by robbers from every side. He found himself unable to return to his home or to continue his journey. He noticed the illusion of the midday from far away and thought it to be a spring of cold water:

"But when he got there, he found it was nothing. There he finds only Allah, Who pays him his account in full. Allah is swift in reckoning." *(24:39)*

There he comes to realise that he was deceived by the shining mirage. This disgrace and that pleasure are not equal in value, to be taken by a learned and experienced person in exchange. There is a cover on the eyes which does not allow noticing the difference between the places of safety and destruction. The hearts are dominated by heedlessness and unaware of the deception.

"It is not people's eyes that are blind, but their hearts within their breasts." *(22:46)*

Another example of transgression is to go beyond what is allowed of eating the dead animal to eat his fill. He was allowed to eat to save his life according to one view of Ahmad, and al-Shafi'i and Abu Hanifah. Imam Malik allowed to eat his fill and to take some with him if he needed. However, if he was not in need and used it to save his money it is transgression. Allah said:
"But if anyone is forced to eat such things by hunger, rather than desire or excess, he commits no sin. Allah is the Most Forgiving, the Most Merciful." *(2:173)*

The words 'al-ithm' and 'al-'udwan' carry the same meaning as 'al-ithm' and 'al-baghy' cited in chapter 7: 33. However, 'al-baghy' is mostly used in reference to the rights of people and treating them unjustly. If 'al-baghy' is joined with 'al-'udwan' the former will mean dealing with the people in what is forbidden in itself, such as stealing, telling lies, accusing falsely and taking initiative in causing harm. 'Al-'udwan' on the other hand will indicate to transgress the limit in recovering the dues. 'Al-baghy' and 'al-'udwan' are in connection to the rights of the human beings, as 'al-ithm' and 'al-'udwan' are in relation to the limits of Allah.

Here there are four things: the rights of Allah, which have their limits, the rights of the human beings, which also have their limit. 'Al-baghy', 'al-'udwan' and 'al-zulm' mean to go beyond the limits, or to fall short of them.

IMMORALITY

Al-Fahsha' means outrageously referring to an abominable act or behaviour. It's evil is obvious to everyone, and every man of reason considers it loathsome. That is why it is used for adultery and sodomy. Allah has called them as 'fahishah' because of their utmost shamelessness. Foul speech, such as abusing and accusing, is called *fuhsh*.

Al-Munkar means unacceptable, meaning an act which is rejected by reason and instinct. It is like a bad smell to the nose, an ugly scene to the eye, a detested food to the tongue and an ugly sound to the ear. Anything which is disliked by reason and senses is outrageous.

Al-Munkar is something which is not known and recognised by the senses, and something which is distasteful is *al-Fahishah*. Ibn Abbas said, "Al-Fahishah is adultery and al-Munkar is something which is not known in the Shari'ah or the Sunnah."

Realise his differentiating between an unknown virtue, which people do not recognise, and that whose ugliness is established in the reasons.

TO SPEAK ABOUT ALLAH WITHOUT KNOWLEDGE

Speaking something about Allah without knowledge is the most serious crime and greatest sin. For this reason it has been mentioned in the fourth level among the forbidden matters on which all the religions have agreed. It is not allowed in any case, and is totally forbidden. It is not like a dead animal, or the blood and the flesh of a swine, which are allowed in particular situations.

To clarify the matter, it should be known that the prohibited things are of two kinds: One that is permanently prohibited and is not allowed in any situation, and the other which is temporarily forbidden in a particular situation. Allah spoke about the permanent forbidden things in the following verse:
"Say, 'My Lord only forbids disgraceful deeds - whether they be open or hidden - and sin and unjustified aggression."

Then He moved to what was more serious:
"And that you, without His sanction, associate things with Him."

He further mentioned what was an even greater sin:
"And that you say things about Allah without knowledge." *(7:33)*

So it is the most serious prohibited matter, because it implies telling lies about Allah and attributing unsuitable things to Him. It also includes changing His religion, denying what He has established and approving what He has rejected, affirming what He has declared as false and discarding what He has affirmed. It further means taking as enemy whom He has declared to be a friend, loving the one whom He hates and hating the one whom He loves and describing Him inappropriately regarding His being, attributes, statements and deeds.

There is no greater sin among the prohibited matters more serious than this. As a matter of fact, this is the root of association of partners with Allah and disbelief. All kinds of innovations and errors are based on it. Every misleading innovation in religion emerges from speaking about Allah without knowledge. Because of its seriousness the early scholars and Imams condemned it unreservedly. They gave warning against its miscreants in every part of the earth and highlighted their misdeeds extensively. They went to the extreme in condemning it more than they did concerning disgraceful deeds, aggression and injustice. It was because the harm caused by innovations and their role in demolishing the religious principles are calamitous. Allah Almighty has condemned the person who declared something permissible or forbidden without having any evidence from Allah. He said:
"Do not say falsely, 'This is lawful and this is forbidden,' inventing a lie about Allah: those who invent lies about Allah will not prosper." *(16:116)*

Then what will be the situation of a person who assigned attributes to Allah which He did not, or denied what He had affirmed about Him.

Some early scholars said, "You should be careful in saying that Allah has allowed this and Allah has prohibited that." Allah says, "You are telling lie, I did not allow this and did not forbid that."

It is very dangerous to declare a thing lawful or forbidden by one's opinion without having any proof from Allah.

The basis of disbelief and shirk is to say something about Allah without knowledge. A polytheist thinks that the object which he has taken as God, apart from Allah Almighty, will bring him nearer to Allah. It will intercede for him, and Allah will fulfil his needs through it, as it happens with kings. Every polytheist says things about Allah without knowledge. In contrast with that not every person who speaks about Allah is a polytheist because it includes declaring Allah without power (ta'til) and innovation, which is a part of shirk.

This explains why speaking about the Messenger of Allah ﷺ is considered to be a path to Hell, because it can involve saying things about Allah without knowledge. What is ascribed to the Messenger is ascribed to the One Who sent him.

"Who could be more unjust than someone who invents a lie against Allah?" *(6:93)*

The offences of the people of innovations are entirely covered in this category and therefore their repentance will not be correct without abandoning the innovation. How can the repentance of a person involved in innovation be valid, who does not realise that it is an innovation, or regards it a Sunnah and calls people to follow it. His misdeeds will not be clear to him unless he is thoroughly acquainted with the Sunnah by exploring and studying it. You will not find a man involved in innovation doing this. The Sunnah itself erases and wipes out innovation. When the sun of the Sunnah shines in the heart of a servant, it takes out the mist of every innovation from it and removes all darkness. The power of darkness (innovation) cannot stand before the power of the sun (Sunnah). A person may not be able to see the difference between the Sunnah and innovation and get out of the darkness of innovation to the light of the Sunnah without adhering to it and moving his heart exclusively to Allah. He seeks support from Allah with sincerity and takes refuge in His Messenger, trying to acquire the knowledge of his sayings and deeds and his character. It is a kind of migration.

"So the one whose migration is to Allah and His Messenger, his migration is to Allah and His Messenger."

Anyone who moves to other than them, it will be his share and portion in the world and the Hereafter. Allah's help is to be sought.

CHAPTER SEVEN
SPECIFIC RULING OF REPENTANCE FOR SPECIFIC CASES

REPENTANCE RULES GOVERNING MISSED OBLIGATORY PRAYER (SALAH)

If a person is unable to pay back the dues which he violated, but repents, what is the status of his repentance? It could happen concerning both the rights of Allah and the rights of the people. An example regarding the right of Allah is the case of a man who deliberately neglected his prayers (salah), whilst being aware of its obligation to pray, and then felt regretful and repented.

This case is disputed among the early scholars. Some of them said that his repentance was enough by expressing regret and resuming the obligatory prayers and performing the missed ones. This was the view of the four Imams and others.

Others have said that his repentance is to resume the prayer in future, and the redoing of the missed ones is not acceptable. It is, therefore, not required of him. This is the view of the Literalists and is reported from some of the earlier scholars as well.

THE OPINION IN FAVOUR OF PERFORMING MISSED OBLIGATORY PRAYER (SALAH)

The people holding the view that redoing the missed prayer is obligatory, base their view on the saying of the Messenger of Allah ﷺ, "Anyone who slept and missed a prayer or forgot it should perform it when he remembers it."

1. They said that if performing the missed prayer is required of the ones who slept or forgot, although, without negligence, it is more necessary for the one who missed it deliberately and by negligence.

2. They further argued that this person had two duties: to perform the prayer and to do it in its time. If he neglected one, he is required to carry out the second one.

3. They contended further that if we say that performing the missed prayer is incumbent by the first command, then it is obvious, but if we say that it is required by a new command, the command of forgetful and sleeping persons are a reminder to the one who missed their prayers intentionally.

4. Moreover, they maintained that if a person is unable to achieve the benefit of an action in full, then he should get as much as possible. Now the benefit of the action in time has been

missed so he should be asked to do it outside of the time.

5. They also argued that the Messenger ﷺ said, "When I order you to do something, do it as much as you can."

Here it is possible for the person to do it outside the time when he was unable to do it in its time. He is therefore required to do what is in his power.

6. They also argued that is it wrong to think that the Shari'ah will allow the man who missed an obligatory act deliberately and committed disobedience of Allah and His Messenger, with an opportunity to redress, yet would not provide the same facility to the one who missed by some excuse.

7. Another argument forwarded by these people is that prayer outside the time is a substitute for performing it in its time. If an act of worship has a substitute and the original was not performed then the person has to move to the substitute. The clear examples are Tayammum with ablution, performing a prayer sitting rather than standing, or lying down when sitting is not possible, and feeding of a poor person instead of fasting due to old age and illness, etc. There are many other examples of such cases.

8. They further argued that performing prayer is a duty fixed with time, but to delay it from its time will not lead to its abolishment, such as delaying the paying back of a loan.

9. Another argument forwarded by them is that the person committed a sin by delaying the prayer but it does not mean he is not required to do it. It is like zakat, when a person delays its payment, or when a person delays the performance of pilgrimage - he commits a sin, but still has to do it.

10. They forwarded another case, that if a man missed the Friday prayer with the Imam he has committed a sin, but is still required to perform Zuhr prayer in its place. It is like performing Fajr prayer after sunrise.

11. They gave another example: The Prophet ﷺ delayed the 'Asr prayer on the occasion of the event of Ahzab and performed it after sunset. It means that prayer can be done out of the time with an excuse or without excuse as some of the Companions did on the occasion of Banu Qurazah.

12. They also said that if performing the prayer outside of the fixed time was not correct and not obligatory, the Prophet ﷺ would not have asked his followers to delay the 'Asr prayer till they had reached their destination. Some of them did it on the way and others did it late in the

night. The Prophet did not blame anyone of them, as both exercised their *ijtihad*.

13. They argued further that every person has a way of repentance. How then can this man be barred from it and made to bear the sin of missing the prayer? This is not in line with the rules of the Shari'ah, which is based on wisdom and mercy, and which takes care of the interest of the people in this life and the Hereafter.

This is all that is said in support of the view, that if a person has missed prayers deliberately, his repentance requires him to perform them later.

OPINION AGAINST PERFORMING MISSED OBLIGATORY PRAYER (SALAH)

Another group believe that for such a person it is not necessary to perform the missed prayer; as it will not be accepted from him. He has to turn to Allah in repentance and resume performing prayers from then on. They have supported their view with the following arguments:

1. When an act of worship is commanded to be performed in a particular way or at a specific time, it will not be accepted unless it is performed in the prescribed manner, at its time and with all the conditions. To delay a prayer from its stated time is like performing it facing a direction other than the Qiblah, prostrating on the cheek instead of the forehead or sitting on the knees instead of bowing for ruku', and so on.

2. Religious duties which are fixed to particular times can only be correct if performed at those times, as are duties that are fixed to specific places. If a person moves them from their places, they will not be valid. The best example here is the places of the pilgrimage: the Plain of Arafat, Muzdalifah, Mina, Safa and Marwah and the Ka'bah. To perform acts prescribed to these places in other places is not acceptable. Changing the timing is like changing places. They will not be accepted if timing is changed.

3. Moving the prayer from its specified time to another time is like moving the staying in Arafat to Muzdalifah or moving the months of pilgrimage from what is stated to other months.

4. What difference is there between the one who moved fast of Ramadan to Shawwal and the one who performed 'Asr prayer at midnight or performed the pilgrimage in Muharram? How will this man's fasting and prayer be correct, but not that man's pilgrimage? Both have violated the command of Allah, the Most High, and committed a sin.

5. Duties assigned by Allah which are set for specific times are not acceptable to Allah in other times. They are not valid before their time and after their time has passed.

6. The duties of the day are not accepted in the night, and those of the night are not valid in the daytime. Abu Bakr al-Siddiq said in his instruction to 'Umar b. al-Khattab, which he and the rest of the Companions agreed, "Allah, the Great, has assigned duties to be performed in the night which He will not accept at daytime as He has assigned duties to be done in the daytime which will not be accepted in the night."

7. The religious duty performed outside its prescribed time is not the same duty, it is something different. If 'Asr prayer is performed after sunset, it is not 'Asr, and its performer did not fulfil his duty. He performed four rak'ahs in the form of the 'Asr prayer, but it is not 'Asr.

8. It is reported through authentic sources that the Prophet ﷺ said, "Whoever missed 'Asr prayer his good deeds are spoiled."

In another version he said, "If one who misses the 'Asr prayer, it is as though his family and wealth have been taken away from him." If it was possible for him to amend his negligence by doing the prayer at another time, his family and wealth would not have been destroyed.

9. The prayer performed after its time is rejected, so it is not proper to say that it is correct and accepted. The Messenger ﷺ said, "Any action which is not in accordance with our practice is rejected."

In another version, he said, "If something is done which is not in line with our practice, it will be rejected."

It shows that this prayer is rejected as it is incorrect, and therefore won't be accepted.

10. Time is a condition for the fulfilling of a duty. It is required for the correctness of the act and completing the duty, like other conditions such as cleanliness, facing the Qiblah, and covering the open parts of the body. The order includes all the conditions. How can there be difference between these conditions while all of them are the same in importance?

11. Those who consider performing the prayer after the passing of the correct time have got no evidence from the text or consensus or correct analogy. We will refute any argument on the basis of analogy and expose its falsehood.

12. It is reported in the Musnad of Imam Ahmad on the authority of Abu Hurayrah ﷺ that the Messenger of Allah ﷺ said, "If a person misses fast of one day deliberately, the fast of the whole lifetime will not compensate it." How can one then say that fasting on another day will be enough?

13. If the validity of the worship depends on the conformity with the command, then this act is not in conformity with the command, and so it is not correct. If we explain the fulfilment by being free of the duty, it will be so when it is done according to the commanded manner. Here it was not done in that manner and as such it is not correct. If it is explained with freedom from the responsibility, then this act did not do it. There is no evidence to prove that such a person fulfilled his duty the way he was commanded.

14. The correct worship is that which the Lawgiver accepts and approves, and this can be known only by his statement or by conformity with His command. Neither is available here, so it can't be declared correct.

15. Validity or invalidity of an action is a legal ruling which can be decided by the Lawgiver alone. What He declared to be valid, or what we know was done in accordance with His order, or was similar to what He declared correct, will be considered so. But in this case all these conditions are missing. The most incorrect argument is to consider it similar to the act which was delayed for an excuse or for permissible reason. This is a wrong argument based on the opposition of the reality and religious norms.

16. The argument on the basis of the following statement of the Prophet ﷺ is not valid:
"Whoever sleeps through a prayer or forgets it, he should do it when he remembers."

Here it can be argued that the Prophet ﷺ ordered doing it later and that the same can be applied in the case of the one who missed it. This argument is invalid because the Prophet ﷺ stipulated that the missing of the prayer was due to sleeping through the time, or due to forgetfulness. Something attached to a condition will not be valid when the condition is not met. It is also reported that the Prophet ﷺ said, "There is no blame in sleep, the blame lies with wakefulness and to delay the prayer till the time of the next prayer enters."

17. This person did not delay his prayer from its time - it was still time when he woke up or remembered. Look at the statement of the Prophet ﷺ, "Whoever slept through a prayer or forgot it, he should perform it when he remembers. That is its time".

Allah, the Most High, says:
"And keep up the prayer so that you remember Me." *(20:14)*

Many commentators explained the last word as 'at the time of remembering Me.'

18. The Prophet ﷺ did perform the morning prayer on the day of the valley after sunrise.

19. Times are of three kinds:

a. One, for a capable and awake person who has no excuse and remembers his duty.

b. The second is for the one who is awake and remembers but has a valid excuse. For him the time of Zuhr and 'Asr prayers are one and the time of Maghrib and 'Isha' is one. He has three times. When this man delays the Zuhr prayer and performs it at the time of 'Asr, he has done it in its time.

c. The third is for the person who was sleeping or forgot. His time is not fixed but he will do the prayer when wakes up or remembers. This is the time for him. This is what the texts of the Shari'ah and its rulings tell us.

The man who neglected prayers deliberately is out of these categories and is the fourth category. To which category would he belong?

20. Allah, glory belongs to Him, has ordained that those who have missed the fasts of Ramadan due to valid reasons such as menstruation, travelling or illness, must keep these fasts at another time. He, the Most High, did not ordain them for someone who missed the fasts without any excuse. There is no indication for this in the Divine Texts. The only thing you can do is base his case on the man with excuses, which is incorrect because the rulings of the Shari'ah make a difference between the two. The Prophet 鈥 has declared that the fast of the whole period will not be enough, let alone a fast of one day.

21. There is also an argument that the person had two duties: 'to perform the religious duty and to do it in its prescribed time. If he missed one of them, the other remained for him to do. This will work in the case where one of the matters is not connected with the other as a condition. For example for a man who was commanded to perform pilgrimage and pay zakat and he carried out one of them, he will not be exempted from the other. But when one thing is a condition for another and he failed to fulfil that condition, then it will not be possible for the other to be accomplished. How can one say that he is ordered to do the other without its conditions and descriptions? Where is there any evidence for it?

If we say that redoing is commanded by a new order, there is no new order in this case. If we say that it was required by the first order, it will be possible when it is useful and its benefit is like the benefit of performing the duty in time, such as making up the fasts of the sick or travelling person, or of the woman on her monthly period, or the person who became unconscious, or slept or forgot. In case the making up is not enough to free the person from the responsibility and the person is not excused by delaying the obligatory act from its time, it is included neither in the first order nor in the second.

22. Another argument is that if a deed's full advantage is not possible to achieve, then only

the possible portion should be acquired. This will be applied when the achievement of the advantage is not attached to a condition, which if not fulfilled, the advantage cannot be achieved. Here there are other ways of gaining the advantage, such as repentance, performing plenty of supererogatory works and good deeds.

23. The argument based on the following saying of the Messenger ﷺ is going too far: "When I order you to do something, do as much as you can."

This statement indicates that when a person fails to carry out all that is required, he should do as much as he can - for instance if a man is unable to stand in prayer, or perform full ablution, or read the whole opening chapter, or to spend the full quota of what is obligatory for him, he will do as much as he can and the rest will be forgiven. But if a person misses an obligatory deed deliberately without any excuse until its time passes, he is not covered in this Hadith. If he was to be included then the Prophet ﷺ would not have warned him of the destruction of his deeds and compared him with a person whose family and wealth have been taken away.

24. By saying that it is not believable that the Shari'ah will be so lenient for this man who deliberately neglects his duty as not to enjoin him to do the missed deeds, and enjoin the excused one to carry it out, is a statement far from reality and completely false. The excused one does his duty in its time and in this he is like the one who has no excuse, and performed his duty in its time. We cannot exempt the deliberately neglectful person from his obligation to relieve him, but because it is of no use to him. He is not commanded for it and it is not going to be accepted from him.

25. There is also the argument that prayer outside of its prescribed time is a substitute to performing it in its time. When the original is not possible, the substitute will take its place. This is only a claim and the dispute is exactly about this. What proof is there that there is an alternative to this deliberately neglectful act? Being a substitute can only be known by the Shari'ah in cases such as Tayammum being the substitute for ablution, or feeding a poor person in case of being unable to fast. In this case, where is the proof that the Shari'ah has made the performing of a missed deed a substitute for performing at the appointed time? This is a false argument.

26. There comparison between praying the missed prayer after its time, to the settlement of a loan after it was due, is not correct. The settlement was restricted by timing, but here the performance of the prayer was required immediately, such as the performance of the pilgrimage or payment of zakat. Time is a condition on these acts and it is unthinkable to do them after the prescribed time. It is to be performed at the beginning of the time, but delaying it does not mean that it is considered missed.

It could be questioned how the making up of a fast of Ramadan is correct, because it is to be done before the next Ramadan. It is not proper to delay it until the next Ramadan. However, if a person delays it still he has to fast and feed a poor person for every day missed. This is the opinion of the Companions of the Prophet, and it shows that the religious act prescribed to the fixed time could be done after the passing of the assigned time.

The answer is that the Shari'ah has differentiated between the days of Ramadan and the days of making up the missed fast. The days of Ramadan are fixed from both sides; no fast is valid before its time or after it. This is not the case with making up. Allah, the Most High, said:

"You who believe, fasting is prescribed for you, as it was prescribed for those before you, so that you may be heedful of Allah. Fasting is for a specific number of days, but if one of you is ill, or on a journey, then (equal number of days to be made) on other days later." *(2:183-184)*

Here Allah Almighty left open the days of making up, and did not fix them. It means that it could be done at any time. There is no evidence in the Qur'an or the Sunnah or the consensus of the scholars that the missed fast is to be done on specific days beyond which it will not be valid.

There is the report of 'A'ishah ﷺ who said, "Sometimes I had to make up fasts of the missed days of Ramadan, but I only got the chance to do it in Sha'ban, because of being busy with the Messenger of Allah, Allah's blessing and peace be upon him."

However, it does not show that the time is fixed between two Ramadans, as the days of Ramadan are fixed between two moons. To compare one with the other is not right. Allah made the days of Ramadan limited, which are not to be altered, but the days of making up are flexible.

Through argument and evidence presented, it is clear that if a person misses a day of Ramadan deliberately, he will not be able to bring another day in its place, but if he misses a day of making up, he may substitute another day for it.

The core of the difference is that the person with a valid excuse has the option to fast any day, but the one who has no excuse must fast the days of Ramadan.

27. As for the person who did not perform Friday prayer, he will have to do the Zuhr prayer instead, because he has to perform one of the two prayers at that time - the Friday or the Zuhr. If he could not do the Friday prayer but the time of Zuhr was still available, he would still be responsible for the duty of the time. This is obvious in the view of the people who consider Friday prayer as a substitute for Zuhr. When the Friday prayer is missed, performing Zuhr would be mandatory.

28. The case of the Prophet ﷺ in delaying the 'Asr prayer till the sunset on the occasion of the battle of the Trench is disputed among the scholars. Some say that it was abrogated. In Imam Ahmad, Malik and al-Shafi'i's' views this was before the prayer of the fear was enjoined. When it was done, delaying of the prayer was cancelled. The delaying is like delaying for the purpose of combining the two prayers and as such it cannot be taken as evidence for abandoning the prayer deliberately. The difference between the two is like the difference between the delaying of the person who slept or forgot and the one who neglected deliberately. Sometimes delaying is required, as is delaying of Maghrib on the night of Muzdalifah.

The second opinion concerning the case of delaying prayer at the time of the battle of Trench is that it is not abrogated and still valid. A warrior has option of delaying his prayer when he is engaged in fighting, and making it up when he is able to. This is the view of Abu Hanifah and is also reported from Ahmad.

In either case, to compare delaying of prayer by a person who abandoned it deliberately with the aforementioned situation is not appropriate. The case of the Companions in delaying the 'Asr prayer on the occasion of the event of Banu Qurayzah is the same as it was ordered by the Prophet ﷺ. Some Companions considered the order and delayed it while others looked at the implication and did it on their way.

The religious scholars are not in agreement about which of the groups was right. Some say that if we were with the people we would have done it on the way, because the intention of the Prophet ﷺ was to incite the marcher to speed up. They compromised between doing the prayer in its time and meeting the enemy in combat. They were more intelligent because they joined the obedience and ijtihad with speeding to the enemy and understood the purpose of the order of the Prophet.

Other scholars have said that if we were with them we would have delayed the prayer like some did. They followed the order of Allah in delaying it because it was obligatory. They were fortunate to stick with the order and acquired double reward. The Prophet ﷺ did not rebuke them because they exercised ijtihad and intended to obey Allah and His Messenger. They will receive only one reward and they are like the judge who exercises his discretion and misses the right point.

29. It could be argued that this man is repentant and regretful. How can the door of repentance be closed in his face, and he be made to bear the sin?

We seek refuge in Allah from closing the door which Allah, the Most High, has opened for all of His sinful servants and which will not be closed until the sun rises from the west. The question is concerning the way of the repentance and its reality, and whether he has to make up the missed prayers or to resume the acts afresh. His case is like a disbeliever who embraced Islam, who is to start his duties and make repentance. To abandon an obligatory duty is not comparable with rejecting Islam with all its duties and obligations. If the repentance of a disbeliever is accepted and he is not required to perform the duties he missed during his disbelief, the repentance of the person who missed prayers without making them up is more deserving of acceptance of his repentance.

THE CASE OF A PERSON WHO FINDS IT DIFFICULT TO REDRESS THE HARM

It may be conceived regarding the rights of the human being in the following cases:

1. If someone unlawfully took away the property of another, then he repented, but it was difficult for him to return the taken property to its owners or their heirs, because he did not know them or they had perished, or for any other reason, what is the status of his repentance?

Some scholars have said that this man's repentance will not be valid until he redresses the harm he did to the people. If it is not possible then his repentance is not possible and he will have to face recompensation on the Day of Judgement.

They argued that it was the right of the person from whom the property was taken, and Allah Almighty will not leave out anything of His servants' rights. He will take them in full without forgoing any bit. The wronged person must take his due from the wrongdoer, even if this is a slap or an abusive word or hitting by a stone.

They said that the best this man can do is to do as many good deeds as he can, so that he is able to make repayment on the Day when no Dinar or Dirham will be available. It is better for him to engage in deeds that will be useful to him on that Day. One useful matter for him is to have patience at the harm of others caused by slandering or accusing. He should not retaliate in this world and not behave in a similar way, so that he is able to refer to his opponent when his good deeds are finished. As he is required to pay back what he has taken from others, his dues will also be given back to him. They may be equal in this regard, or less, or more.

Then the scholars disputed the ruling about the property which is still in his possession. Some of them said that he should not use it at all. Others have said that he should surrender it to the Imam or his deputy, as the custodian of such things. He can then keep it and it would be considered as lost property.

Some other scholars have said that the door of repentance is open for this man, which Allah has not closed for anyone. His repentance includes giving that money in charity on behalf of the owners. On the Day of requital the owners will have the option of accepting his act of charity, and get the reward for that, or to not accept it and instead take from the good deeds of the person, in proportion of their money. The reward of the charity in this case will go to the man who spent it because Allah Almighty is not going to destroy the reward of it. He will give the reward of it to the man who gave it in charity and make him pay back to the person whose wealth he had taken from his good deeds.

This is the view of a group of the Companions, as reported from Ibn Mas'ud, Mu'awiya and Hajjaj b. al-Sha'ir. It is reported that Ibn Mas'ud purchased a slave girl from a man and went inside to fetch the price. The owner of the girl left. Ibn Mas'ud waited, until he lost hope, for the owner to return, but he did not. He then gave the amount of the price in charity and said: 'O Allah, this is from the owner of the slave, if he agrees then the reward is for him, otherwise it is for me and he can take from my good deeds in proportion to the price.'

A man once dishonestly took from some booty, then regretted taking it, and brought what he had taken to the commander of the army. However, he refused to take it, saying *how will I give it to the soldiers who have dispersed*? The man went to Hajjaj b. al-Sha'ir and told the story. Hajjaj said to him, "Allah knows the names of every soldier and their families. Give one fifth to the man in charge of it and give the rest in charity. Allah will make it reach them." He acted upon this advice. When Mu'awiya was told about the incident, he said, "If I had given this opinion, it would have been better to me than half of my kingdom."

2. The same principle applies to articles that are found when their owners were not known, and when the person who found them is not interested in keeping them, he can give them away in charity. If the owner turns up, he will give him the choice of compensation or reward.

This is because the unknown is thought of as nonexistent in the Shari'ah. When the owner is not known he is considered as nonexistent. The owner of this property is not known and it is not appropriate to abandon it as it includes harm for its owner and the poor and for the person who holds it. The owner is harmed because he could not use it and it is the same for the poor people. The one holding it cannot be exempted from the sin and will have to compensate for it on the Day of Judgement. This is not allowed in any Shari'ah, let alone to command it. The religious rulings are based on the benefits of the people and reducing harm as much as possible. To abandon this property and not to use it is an evil act, of which there is no benefit for anyone.

They also said that the rulings of the Shari'ah are established on customary permission, such as the spoken one. So, if a man noticed someone's property in some sort of danger, such as an animal which is about to die and he is able to slaughter it to bring benefit to its owner, the custom allows him to do so. He did it for the sake of its owner and is not liable to him. The same applies to the case of a man whose property was taken away illegally by an unjust man, and he agreed with him to spare some for the owner who was not around, or found it being destroyed so he sold it and kept the price for the owner. In all these cases the custom gives the man permission to act on behalf of the owner. 'Urwah b. al-Ja'd al-Barqi who was appointed by the Messenger ﷺ as his agent, sold the property of the Prophet without his permission and purchased by some of the money he received what he was instructed to buy. When he came to the Prophet with the money and the commodity, the Messenger ﷺ accepted it and blessed him.

This case posed a problem for some jurists, who objected on the grounds that such a person does not take or give possession, whereas the man in the above case did.

Some other scholars contended that he was a full agent in every transaction. This view is more illogical than the first one. It is not known that the Messenger of Allah ﷺ ever appointed a man with full authority. There is no evidence in this respect.

The correct view is that it is based on the ruling that the customary permission is like verbal permission. If a person has agreed with someone to act on his behalf and the price of the commodity went out of his possession, he would be more satisfied to get the price from him.

It is like an ill person whose companions are unable to receive his permission to take out some of his money for his treatment, yet are scared of calamity - they will take out his money, where necessary, without his permission. This is a customary matter. There are many other cases which are based on the benefit of the people, and no religion will prohibit it.

Once it is established, then it is well known that this person who was unable to benefit from his property will be pleased to receive its benefit in the Hereafter. He would not like to waste it and leave it without any benefit in the world or the Hereafter. If he gets the reward in the Hereafter, he will be extremely pleased, much more than if he received it in the world. How can it be said that leaving this money without giving benefit of it to the poor or allowing the one who holds it is better than spending it in religious matters? What kind of benefit is there in leaving that money without use? This is pure viciousness.

A man said to our Shaykh Ibn Taymiyyah that when he was a young boy he ran away from his owner. Now that he knew about him, he considered himself a slave. He said that he wanted to free himself from the responsibility of the due of his owner. He asked many religious people and they asked him to go and sit in the warehouse. Our Shaykh laughed at this opinion and told the man, "Give a best value (price) of yourself in charity on behalf of your master. You do not need to sit in the warehouse without any benefit, only causing harm to yourself. There is no benefit for your master in this, nor for you or the Muslim Community."

The second point is as follows:

When a person has made an illegal deal with someone, such as an adulteresses or a singer, or the seller of wine or a person who gives false witness, and so on, and received money in return, then repented while the money is still in his hand, what can he do?

One group has said that he should return it to its owner because it belongs to him and it was not taken legally, nor did the owner gain any legal profit out of it.

In some other people's opinions, his repentance is by giving it in charity and he should not return it to the one from whom he took it. This is the view of Shaykh al-Islam Ibn Taymiyyah. This is the most correct view. The person took the money with the consent of the owner, who had taken full compensation for it. How can he be allowed to take the commodity and the return together? How can the man take back the money which he used in the disobedience of Allah? It is merely supporting him on his sins and transgressions. Is it proper in the Shari'ah to judge that the adulterer receive all the money which he gave to the woman with whom he committed the sin? It will mean giving his money back while he has taken the benefit.

Suppose that the receiver did not take the money, but that it went out of the possession of the owner to the possession of the person who took, and he received the return. How can one say that his ownership is still intact and he should be given it back? It is unlike the order of giving it in charity. In this case he took it in an illegal way, which its owner agreed to give with his own consent, and he spent it. The best way will be to spend it in a manner which is beneficial to the one who took it. It will not help the culprit and there cannot be a compromise of the two matters.

The repentance of a man whose money is mixed between lawful and unlawful, where it is difficult to distinguish between the two, should be treated in the same way. He should give the quantity of the unlawful portion in charity so that the remaining money becomes pure. Allah knows best.

If a person illegally took some money from someone and the owner died, he has to return it to his inheritor. If the inheritor has also died, then he should return it to *his* inheritor, and so on. If he fails to do so the demand in the Hereafter will be for the real owner because it was his money which was taken away. There is another view that the demand will be for the last inheritor because the right was transferred to him. These are two views in the school of Imam al-Shafi'i.

It could be said that the demand would be for the real owner *and* for each of the inheritors. All of them have a right over it. If he did not surrender it to them then the demand will shift to the Hereafter.

It could also be questioned how the man could get rid of the rights of all of them by repentance. The answer is that he should give the money on their behalf in areas where the reward will reach them. If years have passed and it was possible for the owner to invest that money and make profit, his repentance requires him to give out that amount which he caused the owner to lose. However, if he has made a profit, the whole profit should go to the real owner. This is the view of al-Shafi'i and Ahmad. Abu Hanifah and Malik said that the profit would go to the person who took it illegally.

There is a third view that both the owner and the snatcher will share it. This is reported by Imam Ahmad and chosen by our Shaykh Ibn Taymiyyah. It is the most appropriate view. So, a portion of the profit will be added to the real money and given in charity.

The same applies to the case where a man robbed a she-camel or a goat and it produced offspring - all of them will belong to the real owner. If the mother or any of the offspring died he would have to return the price of the mother and the dead ones. This is the view of Imam al-Shafi'i and of the followers of Ahmad. Imam Malik said that if the mother died, its owner has the choice of taking the price of the day she died and leaving the offspring for the robber or he can take the offspring and forsake the price. There is a third view that he will pay the value of the mother and keep half of the offspring. Allah knows best.

IS THERE A SIN FOR WHICH THERE IS NO REPENTANCE?

Is there a sin for which there is no repentance? There is a dispute amongst the scholars about this. The majority of scholars hold the view that repentance can wash away every sin. Repentance can be made for every offence and it is accepted.

Some people say that there is no repentance for a murderer. This is the well known view of Ibn Abbas and a report from Ahmad. Ibn Abbas's companions argued with him saying that Allah, the Most High, said in the Qur'an:

"They do not take a life, which Allah has made sacred, except in the pursuit of justice, nor commit adultery. Whoever does these things will face the penalties: their torment will be doubled on the Day of Resurrection, and they will remain in torment, disgraced, except those who repent, believe, and do good deeds: Allah will change the evil deeds of such people into good ones. Allah is Most Forgiving, Most Merciful." *(25:68-70)*

Ibn Abbas replied to them, saying that this verse was revealed concerning the pre-Islamic period. It so happened that members of the polytheists who had committed murder and adultery came to the Messenger of Allah ﷺ and said, "What you are preaching is good, but tell us whether there is an expiation for what we have done?" So, this verse was sent down, and it deals with those people.

The following verse, which was revealed in Chapter 4 of the Qur'an speaks clearly about the one who murders a believer. Allah, the Most Wise, says:

"If anyone kills a believer deliberately, the punishment for him is Hell, and there he will remain forever. Allah is angry with him, and curses him, and has prepared a tremendous torment for him." *(4:93)*

When a man is aware of the religion of Islam and its rules, and commits murder, his place is in Hell.

Zayd b. Thabit said, 'When the verse number 68 of surah Al-Furqan (25) was revealed, we were surprised by its leniency. We waited for seven months, then the harsh rule was revealed after the soft one, and the first one was abrogated.

Ibn Abbas said that the verse of Chapter 25 was revealed in Makkah and the verse of Chapter 4 was sent down in Madinah and it was not abrogated.

They argued that the repentance of a man who deliberately killed a believer is impossible. It is possible only by asking the affected person to forgive or by returning the soul which he took, back to its body. Both are impossible. How then can his repentance be accepted when he is unable to pay the deceased back his due and did not ask him to forgive?

This is not to compare to the case where money was taken but its rightful owner died and so it was not returned back to him. Here this can be made up by giving charity on his behalf.

One should not raise an objection by saying that the association of a partner to Allah (polytheism or shirk) is more serious than killing, yet repentance from it is possible. Association of partners is the pure right of Allah and thus to repent from it is possible. Any right of a man could be redeemed only by paying to him what he is owed, or by having it exempted from him - and this is not possible.

The majority of scholars have justified their view with the following statement of Allah Almighty:
"Say, My servants, who have harmed themselves by their own excess, do not despair of Allah's mercy. Allah forgives all sins. He is truly the Most Forgiving, the Most Merciful." *(39:53)*

This is concerning the person who repents. They also quoted the following verse:
"Allah will not forgive the joining of partners with Him: anything less than that He forgives to whoever, He will." *(4:48 & 116)*

This is about a man who did not repent. The Almighty made the difference between shirk and sins less than that and attached forgiveness to His will so He made it restricted and conditional.

In the first verse He made it general and left it unlimited.

They also argued by the verse:

"I am Most Forgiving towards those who repent, believe, do righteous deeds, and stay on the right path." *(20:82)*

If this murderer repents, believes, and does good deeds, Allah, the Most High, will forgive him.

They further said that it has been reported through authentic sources that the Messenger of Allah ﷺ mentioned a man who killed a hundred people then he repented, and Allah accepted his repentance and he was joined with the village of the righteous people where he wanted to go.

It is also reported on the authority of 'Ubadah b. al-Samit that the Messenger of Allah ﷺ said in front of a group of the Companions, "Pledge allegiance to me that you will not associate partners with Allah, will not commit theft and adultery, will not kill your children, will not bring forth a slander you have invented between your arms and legs and will not disobey me in what is right. Whoever remains faithful to this will get his reward from Allah. But if anyone committed some of the said offences and was punished in the world, it will be expiation for him. For the one who committed a sin and Allah covered it for him, his fate is with Allah. If He wills, He will forgive him and if He wills, He will punish him." So, the Companions all pledged allegiance on that.

They also argued that the Prophet ﷺ narrated that his Lord, glory and might belong to Him, said, "Son of Adam, if you meet me with so many sins as to fill the earth, but you have not joined a partner to Me, I will meet you with similar forgiveness."

The Prophet ﷺ said, "Whoever dies and he has not associated any partner with Allah will go to Paradise." He also said, "The one whose last words are 'There is no god but Allah' will go to Paradise."

He said in another Hadith, "Allah has forbidden Hell for a man who said, 'There is no god but Allah', seeking the pleasure of Allah."

In the Hadith of the intercession it is said, "Take out from Hell anyone who has mustard seed's weight of faith."

It is also reported that Allah said:

"By My Honour and Greatness I will take out of Hell anyone who said, 'there is no god but Allah.'"

There are many reports in this respect, which clearly indicate that no one of the people of Tawhid will remain in Hell for ever.

As for the verse of the Chapter 4 there are many verses similar to it, for example the saying of Allah, the Most High:
"Those who disobey Allah and His Messenger and overstep His limits will be consigned by Allah to the Fire, and there they will stay forever." *(4:14)*

Allah also said:
"Whoever disobeys Allah and His Messenger will have Hell's Fire as his permanent home." *(72:23)*

Allah also said:
"Those who consume the property of orphans unjustly are actually swallowing fire in their own bellies. They will burn in blazing fire." *(4:10)*

The Messenger ﷺ said, "Whoever kills himself with an iron tool, he will be punished by it forever in Hell Fire."

There are many other statements in this regard. The scholars differed among themselves concerning the application of these statements. Some said that they were to be taken literally and the people who committed the indicated crimes will be put in Hell for ever. This is the view of the *Kharijites* and *Mutazilah*. Then they differed and the *Kharijites* said they were disbelievers as it is the only disbelievers who are going to remain in Hell forever. But the *Mutazilah* said they were not disbelievers but transgressors and will remain in Hell forever. This is when they do not repent.

Some other people said that this warning was in the case of those who commit these crimes thinking of them as permissible, because such a person is a disbeliever. As for the man who did them considering them to be prohibited, he is not included in the warning of remaining in Hell forever, although he will enter it. Imam Ahmad rejected this view saying that if a man considered these crimes to be lawful, he is a disbeliever even though he did not commit them.

A third group said that the argument on the basis of these texts is subject to prove the generality of the words and there are no general words in the language. For this reason those people rejected the general application.

They wanted to obstruct the arguments of the *Kharijites* and the *Mu'tazilah*, but this involves the neutralisation of the whole Shari'ah, rather the suspension of all the reports. They tried to refute a false claim by what was more objectionable. They were like the ones who intended to build a palace yet demolished the whole town.

A fourth group said that there is an omission in the verse, which is common in the Arabic language. Then they differed and one group said that the condition is omitted and the meaning was, 'his recompense is such and such if Allah does it or wills it.' Another group said that exception is dropped, giving the meaning that the person's recompense will be such and such unless Allah forgives. This is a claim without any proof.

A fifth group held the opinion that it is a warning, and to ignore a warning is not blameworthy, but rather praiseworthy. It is alright with Allah to carry out His warning but it is not so concerning His promise. The difference between the two is that a warning is His right and not carrying it out is a forgiveness as a result of His generosity and kindness; whereas the promise is a duty which He has taken upon Himself and Allah never breaks His promise.

They said that Ka'b b. Zuhayr praised the Messenger of Allah ﷺ by this when he said, "I was informed that the Messenger of Allah has issued a warning to me, but the pardon is hoped for with the Messenger of Allah."

Abu 'Amr b. al-'Ala' and 'Amr b. 'Ubayd debated on this issue. 'Amr b. 'Ubayd said, "Abu 'Amr, Allah does not break His promise and He has said, 'Whoever kills a believer deliberately.'" *(4:93)*

Abu 'Amr replied, "Owe unto, 'Amr! You made a mistake because of your incorrect knowledge of Arabic. The Arabs do not consider failing to carry out the warning a matter of disgrace, but it is regarded as generosity and kindness. Did you not hear the saying of the poet, who said, 'My cousin is not scared of my attack as long as I live. He is not afraid of the assault of the warner. When I give warning or make promise to him, I will nor execute my warning, but will fulfil my promise.'"

Another group said that these texts and other similar ones in which the cause of punishment is mentioned do not require the execution of the ruling when the cause is found. The ruling will be applied when the cause is found and there is no impediment. These texts indicate that such-and-such is the reason for punishment, there are impediments either by the text itself or by the consensus of the scholars. Repentance is an impediment by the consensus, and belief in the oneness of Allah is an impediment by many texts which cannot be turned down. Similarly the great good deeds erase the sins and the serious afflictions are also the source of expiation. Applying the prescribed punishment in the world is another factor which obstructs the execution of the punishment. One cannot ignore these texts and both sides of them are to be applied. That is how the parallel is established between the good and evil deeds in considering the cause and obstruction of the punishment, and the more preferable side is to be taken.

This principle is the foundation of the benefits and the harm of the world and the Hereafter, and on it is based the religious rules and the Divine decrees. Allah, glory be to Him, has created an opposite for everything to control matters, and the stronger dominates. Strength, for example, is the cause of health and well being while the disorder of the human infirmity is an impediment to the work of strength. Similar is the case of powers of medicines and illness which combat with one another, one trying to bring about health whilst the other resists it. In the end, the stronger succeeds.

This explains the division of the people between those who will go to Paradise and not to Hell, and those whose fate will be the opposite, and those who will go to Hell and then come out of it after staying there, according to their offences.

A person who is gifted with brilliant discernment can observe all that Allah has described of the affairs of the life, to come as though he sees them with own eyes. He will realise that this is the result of Him being the Lord, His honour and wisdom and being the object of worship. He cannot do anything against it. This person will realise these facts by his mental vision as he watches the sun and the stars with his eyes. This is the perfect faith which burns down the evil deeds, as the fire burns the wood. A man with this quality of faith will never insist on committing evil deeds even if he may slip to them. The light of faith which he has will push him always to turn to Allah in repentance. He is the most beloved of the people to Allah. This is how the texts of the warning should be understood.

THE CASE OF A MAN WHO KILLED SOMEONE AND WAS KILLED IN RETALIATION

The scholars are in disagreement concerning a man who committed murder, then repented and surrendered himself and was killed in retribution: Does the killed person have some dues for him on the Day of Judgment?

A group said that there remains nothing for the deceased person because the retribution was the punishment of the killer. Prescribed punishments are atonements for the offenders. In this case, the inheritors of the man who was killed have taken the dues of their man. They acted on his behalf and it is as though the killed person has taken his right. There is no difference whether the man takes his dues by himself or if his agent does it on his behalf.

Another group said that the killed person was treated unjustly and lost his life. He could not receive his right. The inheritor received his revenge and took his anger out; there was nothing for the killed person.

They said that rights in the case of killing are three:
a. One for Allah
b. The second for the killed person and
c. The third for the inheritor

The right of Allah cannot be fulfilled, except by the repentance. The inheritor has taken his right by retribution. He had three options: retribution, or forgiving, or taking money in compensation. If he forsakes or takes money, the right of the person who was killed is not dropped out. The same will apply if he takes retribution.

They further argued that if the killed person said, "Do not kill him because I want to take my right on the Day of Judgement," but they still killed, will his right be dropped or not. If you say that his right is dropped, it is not true because he did not agree to that. If you say that it was not dropped, how then can you drop it with the retribution, knowing that he did not approve it?

As you can see, these are strong arguments and cannot be refuted, except by similar or stronger evidences.

The correct view - and Allah knows best - is that when the killer repented from the right of Allah and surrendered himself voluntarily to the inheritor to take revenge, both rights will be dropped from him. Only the right of the one who inherited continues, which Allah cannot allow to be dispossessed. The Almighty will make the compensation of the killed person a source of forgiveness for the killer. His plight did not end with the killing of his murderer, and the sincere repentance wipes out all that which was committed before it. Now the killed person will be compensated for his loss and the killer will be forgiven because of his perfect repentance. He becomes like a disbeliever who was engaged in fighting against Allah and His Messenger and killed a Muslim in the battle. Then he becomes a good Muslim: Allah, the most High, will compensate the killed person as a martyr, and forgive the disbeliever because of his Islam. He will not impose blame on him for killing a Muslim unjustly because his repentance destroyed whatever he committed before.

This follows that when the killer surrendered himself and the guardian forgave him and the killer repented sincerely, Allah will accept his repentance and compensate the killed person.

This is what a person of knowledge and understanding can say. However, after all, the judgement is in the hand of Allah.

"Your Lord will judge between them by His judgement; and He is the Exalted in might, the Knowing." *(27:78)*

CHAPTER EIGHT
THE VARIOUS STATES OF HUMAN BEINGS

THE DISTINCT FEATURES OF DISOBEDIENCE AND THE RIGHTEOUS PATH

There are thirteen aspects, some pertaining to disobedience and others leading to the righteous course:

1. The aspect of animal nature and satisfying the lust
2. The aspect of carrying of the requirements of the nature
3. The situation of coercion
4. The aspect of fate or decree
5. The feature of the wisdom
6. The feature of Tawhid
7. The aspects of the Names and the Attributes
8. The features of support and disappointment
9. The feature of belief and its innumerable evidences
10. The situation of mercy
11. The situation of weakness and incapacity
12. The aspect of humility and need
13. The aspect of love and devotion

The first four belong to the deviating people, and the remaining eight are for the people of the right course. The highest aspect is the tenth item, referring to mercy.

This section is the most valuable part of this book and deserved to be held fast. You are unlikely to find this discussion in any other book, except what is mentioned in our book entitled *The manual of two emigrations in the way of two delights.*

1. THE ASPECT OF ANIMAL NATURE AND SATISFYING THE LUST

It is the condition of the ignorant people that they are no different from animals, except that they have an upright posture and power of expression. Their main goal is to satisfy their lust by any means. They have the nature of animals and did not develop to the rank of humanity, let alone reach the rank of the angels. Their condition is too contemptible to be mentioned. Their conditions vary, like different animals whose nature is found in them. Here are some of the examples when humans acquire characteristics of animals:

i. Some of them have a canine nature i.e. dog-like. If they were to discover a corpse that is enough to satisfy thousand of dogs, they would take it and keep it away from other dogs. They will bark at any dog which tries to approach it and will not allow them to benefit from it, without fighting. Their interests lie in filling their bellies with any type of food, whether dead or legally slaughtered, rotten or good. They have no shame concerning any bad matters. If you chase them, they will pant, or if you leave them, they will still pant. If you feed them, they will move their tails and go around you, and if you drive them away, they will bark at you.

ii. There are those who have the nature of a donkey, which is created for labour and fodder. Whenever its fodder is increased its labour increases. It is the dumbest of all animals and has very little understanding. That is why Allah, the Glorious, has cited it as an example for those whom He gave His Book but they did not understand it and follow it. He cited the example of dog for a learned wicked man who was given His signs but he cast it off and clung to the earth and followed his desire. There are great secrets in these two comparisons. But this is not the place to disclose them.

iii. Then there is those men who have the nature of beasts full of anger. They only think about aggression over people, and overpowering them by all means they have in their power. This is instilled in them, the same way that the beast behaves according to what is in its nature.

iv. Then there are the people whose natures are like those of a mouse, who is wicked by his nature and spoils what comes near him. His mute expression says: 'Glory be to the One who created him for mischief.'

v. Yet there are those who have the nature of poisonous reptiles, such as snakes, scorpions and similar insects. This type causes harm by their eyes and make a man to go to the grave and a camel to enter a pot. The eyes alone did not produce that effect; it was the wicked poisonous soul which assumed the nature of anger while having great admiration for envy. It came in contact with their victims, who were unaware and unarmed, and bit them like the snake which looks at the open part of the body of humans, and bites, and the result is either death or pain. The harm of the person of the evil eye does not depend on seeing, but when an absent object is described to him, he can cause him harm. The fault lies with ignorance and heedlessness of the victim, and his being unarmed. Those people with evil eyes cannot affect those people who are well armed. It is like the snake which comes across a man who is armed to the teeth and is unable to find an open part of his body; it will fail to harm him.

It is, therefore, necessary for a man who is interested in keeping his soul safe that he is fully covered by the arms of the war, punctual on repeating the parts of the Qur'an and the Sunnah which provide the protection of Allah ﷻ. When a person is known to cause harm by evil eye, he should be arrested, kept away from the people and given food and drink until he dies. This is the opinion of many jurists and there should not be any dispute in this matter, as it is for the welfare of the Muslims and keeping them away from harm.

Now the question arises - if this man kills someone with his evil eyes, will he be killed in retribution? The answer is that if it was without his free will but he was forced to it, he will not be killed and pay the blood money. If he did it deliberately, knowing that it was going to cause death, the guardian of the deceased has the right to take revenge by causing him similar harm by evil eye. He will not be killed by the sword in retribution because such an act usually does not kill.

One may ask, what is difference between killing by evil eye and killing by magic in which you prescribe retribution by killing? The answer is that there is a difference in two ways:

The first is that the magic which kills is the same in many cases. The people practising this type of magic have various methods to kill.

Secondly, it is not possible to retaliate with a similar act because it is prohibited. It is like killing by sodomy or pushing wine in his throat. In these cases the culprit will be killed by the sword.

vi. There are people who have the nature of swines, which pass by the clean objects and do not pay attention to them, yet devour a human being's excrement. Many people have similar natures, where they watch and hear about many good deeds being performed, exceedingly more so than evil deeds, but they do not speak of them. However, if they notice a mistake or a bad word they make it their delicious subject to mention to everyone.

vii. Some people are like peacocks, that are concerned only with decoration and embellishment.

viii. Others have the character of camels, the most rancorous animal and of rough heart.

ix. There are some who have the feature of bears, which are dumb and vicious.

x. Others have the quality of monkeys.

The animal which has the best character is the horse, which is the noblest and most honourable animal. The same can be said about sheep. Anyone who lives with this kind of animal, acquires their habits and nature. If he eats its meat, the similarity will be higher. For this reason Allah, the Most High, has prohibited eating the meats of beasts and predatory birds because they pass their character to the eater. Allah knows best.

The point is that the people of this aspect have no concern besides their desires, and crave nothing beyond that.

2. REQUIREMENTS OF THE NATURE

This is like the feeling of the heretic doctors and philosophers who believe that mankind is made up of four elements. If these elements are in balance, the body is alright, but if some of these dominate the others, the equilibrium is lost. In the same way, the composition of the human from the body, soul, nature and body liquids & secretions depends on their synchronisation. It cannot be controlled except by inner power or from outside force. Most humans have no inner control and they are in need of something above them, which can keep a balance in their behaviour. It is like their need for food, drink and dress. These philosophers believe that if a person has enough power of understanding which controls his behaviour, he does not need someone else to put his action right.

3. THE CATEGORY OF THE PEOPLE OF COMPULSION (COERCION)

These are the people who believe that they are forced to do their deeds. They are done without their will. Actually they do not believe that these deeds are done by them.

They say that one of them is not in fact working; he has no power to do anything. The one who moves them and works is someone else. He is only a tool; his actions are like the blowing of the wind which moves the trees. When you confront these people with their actions they take refuge in fate and attribute their sins to it. Sometimes they go to the extreme and believe that all their deeds, good and bad, are pious deeds because they are in line with fate and predestination.

They say that compliance with injunction is obedience, and that compliance with fate is also obedience.

They make the will of Allah as a basis for their deeds, and say that since He has destined them, He approves them. These people are worse than those who deny the Divine Decree, and are in direct contradiction of Allah's Books, His Messengers and His religion. Some of them go to the extent of offering excuses for the Devil, feel pity for him and attribute injustice to Allah in dealing with him. They ask what his fault was, because he kept his face safe from prostrating to anyone except the Creator. They say that this was in agreement with the command and will of Allah and that he couldn't bow down because Allah stopped him from doing so. They further state that by refusing to bow down to anyone apart from Allah, he did a good deed.

These are the real enemies of Allah and true friends of the Devil. They are his brothers and companions. You find them lamenting the case of Satan and you may even see amazing types of crying and wailing. They complain about the Devil's fate and accuse the Most Powerful Compeller of doing an injustice to him. You will find them grumbling and groaning in the way which an incapable and overpowered person does when he cannot find a way to deal with his opponent. These are the people about whom Shaykh al-Isla Ibn Taymiyyah said in one of his poems, "The enemies of Allah, the *Qadariyyah,* will be called to Hell on the Day of Resurrection."

4. THE ASPECT OF DIVINE DECREE

The fourth group is that of *Qadariyyah* who do not believe in the Divine Decree. They claim that all the crimes and sins are committed by the people with their free will and not the will of Allah. Allah did not decree them nor write or will. He did not create their deeds. He, the Most High, has no power to guide or misguide anyone except by telling them. He does not inspire man to be on the right path or the wrong one; nor does He lead him to evil or to good deeds.

They claim that there are matters which take place in the kingdom of Allah without His will, and He wills what does not take place. Man is the creator of his own acts, without the will of Allah. Sins and transgressions occur with the will of the people who create them; they are not created by Allah and are not attached to the will of Allah.

These people are very unfortunate; they do not seek help from Allah, or put their trust in Him or hold fast to Him. They do not ask Allah to guide them, to keep their hearts firm from deviating, to support them to do deeds for His pleasure and keep them away from sins. All kinds of troubles happen to them but they claim that they are their own doing and do not fall under the will of the Lord.

Satan has agreed with this much from them, so he does not incite them to disobedience and misdeeds. He has two purposes. Firstly, to establish firmly this belief in their hearts and let them believe that it is the correct one. He tells them that they are keeping away from the major sins, which the followers of the Sunnah commit and that this is a sign that the matter is entrusted to them and it is them who protect themselves from the sins.

Secondly, he makes ignorant people fall prey to them. When they see these people involved in devotion and worship and keeping away from sins which are considered them very serious, others feel that these are the people of truth. Satan loves innovation more than sins and transgression. When he hunts down the ignorant people, he does not urge them to commit sins, because they have fallen into innovation. Instead, Satan will discourage them from committing sins and expose them as bad in their eyes and hearts. These facts are known only to the people who have been granted discernment.

5. THE WISDOM

The fifth feature is the character of the people on the right path. It is the position of wisdom of Allah in His Decree for His servant, for what He disapproves of and hates, and He blames the one who commits it and punishes him. If He wished, He could have averted him from it and saved him. Allah, glory be to Him, cannot be disobeyed by force. There is nothing in the world which can take place without His will.

"All creation and command belong to Him, Exalted be Allah, the Lord of all the worlds" *(7:54)*

These people believe that Allah did not create anything in vain. There is wisdom in all that He has decreed and decided, whether good or bad, obedience or disobedience. The reason cannot comprehend His brilliant wisdom and the tongue cannot express it.

The source of His Decree and decision in what He hates and abhors come from His beautiful name "the Wise". Allah, the Glorious, said to His angels:
"When your Lord told the angels, 'I am going to put a successor on earth.' They said, 'How can you put someone there who will cause damage and bloodshed, when we celebrate Your praise and proclaim Your holiness?' He said, 'I know things you do not." *(2:30)*

Allah Almighty has placed in the sins, transgressions and crimes many signs and wisdom which enables man to recognise Him. They also include signs of His Lordship, greatness, power, full knowledge and being the object of worship alone. The people of good vision see them by the eyes of their hearts and declare:
"Our Lord, You have not created all this without purpose. Glory be to You." *(3:191)*

It is a clear sign of His shining wisdom. There is a witness in every act, of motion and stillness, and in every matter there is evidence that He is One.

How many clear signs are on earth, which indicate the existence of Allah and truthfulness of His Messengers, and prove that meeting with Him is truth? These signs were caused by the disobedience and misdeeds of the sons of Adam. One of them is the flood which drowned the people of Noah in which the water rose above the peaks of the mountains and immersed all the residents of the earth, but Allah saved His friends and the followers of His religion and Tawhid. How many signs and lessons are in it, which will remain until the end of the time? There are similar lessons in the destruction of the people of 'Ad and Thamud.

There are many tokens in the case of Pharaoh and his people from the time Moses came to them until they were drowned. Had they not committed sins and aggression these amazing signs would not have been seen. It is in the Torah that Allah said to Moses, "Go to Pharaoh, I will make his heart hard and bar him from belief so that I can bring out My signs and amazing works in Egypt." And Allah did what He promised because of the aggression of Pharaoh and his people.

Allah also manifested His power in case of Ibrahim ﷺ when He commanded the fire to be cool and safe for him. Due to the violent crimes of his people, Ibrahim was thrown into the fire, which became a sign and honour for Ibrahim to deserve the noblest ever friendship of Allah Almighty.

Many other messengers achieved honour, status, nearness, and prominence with Allah because they exercised patience against the harm of their people who tried to cause them all sorts of trouble.

Allah, the Clement, chooses friends and true servants from among the children of Adam because of their suffering at the hand of their enemies and showing steadfastness for the sake of their Lord. The Almighty left them to undergo the troubles so that He can raise their status and rank.

There is inherent wisdom and numerous benefits that are discovered because of sins and crimes. Allah decreed what He disliked, to bring out what is more beloved to Him. This is another example of Divine Wisdom.

Acquisition of this superb lovable matter is more beloved to Him than missing disliked and hateful affairs. Although the missing of it was desirable to Him, the attainment of this lovable matter which could not have been attained without that hateful matter was more desirable. Missing of this desired matter was more hateful to Him than missing that undesirable and loathsome thing. His perfect wisdom decided to attain the most beloved matter through missing the less desirable one. He did not like to leave out this desirable matter for abandoning the undesirable one. To assume existence of this without that is like assuming the existence of effect without the cause, which is against the perfect wisdom and full power of the Almighty.

The following example will be enough to illustrate the issue: If Adam ﷺ had not committed the mistake of eating from the forbidden tree, the great desirable effects would have not been found. It was because of that mistake that He gave responsibility to His creatures and put them under examination by sending messengers, revealing books and demonstrating His signs and wonders. He arranged this to honour His devoted servants and disgrace His enemies. Here we see His justice, grace, might and revenge, pardoning and forgiving, and giving victory to those who worship Him, love Him, undergo troubles and afflictions for him by performing what He likes while living amongst the hostile people.

Supposing that Adam ﷺ had not eaten from that tree and had not been expelled, nothing of what we mentioned would had taken place. Satan's trick, which was known only to Allah, would not have been seen. In that case the good and the bad would not have been separated. No provision of honour, reward or punishment and disgrace would have been available. There would not have been an abode of happiness and delight, or abode of misery and justice.

How great that His wisdom and complete favour is seen in His giving power to His friends over His enemies, and vice versa? How many desirable things take place in this world? His praises are sung by the people of the heavens and the earth. His devoted servants show humility and affection to Him. They express their need and beg for His help and support, and ask Him not to make them among His enemies. They see that He has deserted them, does not pay attention to them, hates them and has prepared torment for them. All this is by His will and action in His kingdom. His servants are in awe and have great apprehension of Him. They are full of fear and show humbleness to Him. All this would have not been seen if Adam was not expelled from the Heavens.

When the angels witness the Devil and what happened to him, and see the case of Harut and Marut, they place their heads before their Lord in acknowledgement of His greatness, and surrendering to His honour. They are afraid of being driven away from His favour and express their humility and needs to Him, and seek His mercy.

In the same way when His devoted servants witness the conditions of His enemies and His aversion of them, His anger and desertion, they submit themselves to Him in humbleness, lowliness, dejection and great respect. They seek help from Him, turn to Him, and put their trust in Him, having hope and fear of Him. They realise that there is no escape for them except to Him and no one can save them except Him. It is only He who can rescue them from His wrath and redeem them from His torment. All bounty and grace lie in His hands.

This is a drop from His encompassing wisdom. A man of vision and understanding can see beyond that, and discover the wonders of His wisdom, which he cannot express in words.

The share of the servant from the realisation of the Divine wisdom is in accordance with his alertness and power of discernment. It depends on his perfect knowledge and understanding of Allah, his Names and His Attributes. It also requires the recognition of the rights of Lordship and servitude. Every believer has a fixed amount of it and a place which he cannot miss and cannot pass. Allah is the only helper and supporter.

6. TAWHID OR ONENESS OF ALLAH

This requires a person to believe that the Lord Almighty and Most Powerful holds alone the power of creation and command. What He wills takes place, and what He does not will not happen. Not even the smallest creature moves without His permission. All the creatures are under His control. Every heart is between His two fingers; if He wants to keep it straight, it will remain so, but if He wills to make it deviate, it will stray. He moves hearts the way He likes. It is He who granted the piety to the souls of the believers and guided and purified them. He inspired the souls of the rebellious with the wickedness and wretchedness. Whosoever Allah guides, nobody can send him astray, and whosoever He misguides, no one can guide him. He guides whom He wishes by His grace and mercy, and misguides whom He wills by His justice and decree.

Ibn Abbas said, "Belief in Divine Decree is the system of Tawhid. If someone denies the decree, his Tawhid is destroyed and whoever believes in fate, his belief is solid".

In this position the station of the servant with regards to 'Only You we worship and only to You we turn for help' is completed. The foot of the servant stands firm in the Tawhid of Lordship and from there he ascends to the Tawhid of divinity. When a man becomes certain that harm and benefit, giving or holding, guidance and misguidance, happiness and distress, are all in the control of Allah and no one else, he becomes the real servant of Allah. He believes that it is only Allah who turns the hearts and distracts as He wishes. No one but He alone gives help and support to whom He wishes. The unfortunate man is the one whom He has deserted and disgraced. The most correct heart is that which is straight, clean and strong. Whoever takes Allah alone as the being worthy of worship, and puts His love above every other thing, fears Him alone and put hope in Him alone, his love will dominate all other love in his heart. The fear of Allah will overwhelm all other fears, and hope of Him will be above the hope of anything.

This is the indication of the Tawhid of divinity in the heart, which entered it from the gate of Tawhid of Lordship. This is so because the first thing that the heart is attached to is the Tawhid of Lordship, then it ascends to the Tawhid of Divinity. This is how Allah, the Glorious, argues with the disbelievers in His Book. He says that they take Him as the Creator of everything, then demolish it by association of partners in the Tawhid of Divinity.

In this position the station of "only You we worship" is established. Allah Almighty said:
"If you ask them, 'who created them', they will surely say, 'Allah', how then they are so deluded?" *(43:87)*

That is when they ascertain that there is no Lord or Creator other than Allah, then how are they turned away from attesting that there is no god but Allah?

Allah, the Blessed, also said:
"Say, 'Who owns the earth and all who live in it,' if you know? And they will reply, 'Allah'. Say, 'Will you not take heed?' *(23:84)*

If you reflect on this, you will realise that if He alone is the Master of the earth and all that is in it, and He is their Creator, their Lord and the King, then certainly He alone deserves to be worshiped and idolised. As there is no other Lord for them, there is no Divine being to be worshipped by them. In the Qur'an Allah inquires:

"Say, 'Who is the Lord of the seven heavens, and the Lord of the Mighty Throne?' They will reply, 'Allah', say, 'Will you not be mindful?' Say, 'Who holds control of everything in hand? He protects, while there is no protection against Him, if you know?' They will reply, 'Allah', Say, 'Then how can you be so deluded?'" *(23:86-89)*

The same message is conveyed in the following verses from surah An-Naml, The Ant:

"Say (Prophet), 'Praise be to Allah and peace on the servants He has chosen.' Who is better: Allah, or those who they set up as partners with Him? Who created the heavens and earth? Who sends down water from the sky for you - with which We cause gardens of delight to grow: you have no power to make the trees grow in them - is it another god beside Allah? No! But they are people who take others to be equal with Allah. Who is it that makes the earth a stable place to live? Who made rivers flow through it? Who set immovable mountains on it and created a barrier between the fresh and salt water? Is it another god beside Allah? No! But most of them do not know. Who is it that answers the distressed when they call upon Him? Who removes their suffering? Who makes you successors in the earth? Is it another god beside Allah? Little notice you take. Who is that guides you through the darkness on land and sea? Who sends the winds as heralds of good news before His mercy? Is it another god beside Allah? Allah is far above the partners they put beside Him! Who is it that originates creation and reproduces it? Who is it that gives you provision from the heavens and earth? Is it another god beside Allah? Say, 'Show me your evidence then, if what you say is true.'" *(27:59-64)*

Allah argues that the one who did all those things alone is their God. If there is another Lord with Him who did any of the things then it is alright for you to worship him. But if there is no Lord with him who has done that, then how do you make another God to worship?

It is therefore more appropriate to explain the questions in the above verses with 'Is there another God who did this?' so that the argument is complete, and the reply will be 'No'. The meaning of this is that if there is no God except Him, then who created, as He did, and how can you worship other gods beside Him? You assert that the lordship of others is invalid, so their divinity also should be false and invalid.

Some commentators explained the questions in the verses as 'Is there another God with Allah?' without adding 'Who did it?' This explanation is weak for two reasons:

First, they said that there were other gods with Allah. They did not deny it.

Secondly, the argument is not complete and it is not possible to convince them without saying that if you say 'that there is no God who did as He did', then why set up with Him another God who is incapable of creating anything?

It is similar to the statements of Allah in surahs Ar-Ra'd (The Thunder), Luqman, An-Nahl (The Bee) and Al-Furqan (The Criterion):

"Have the partners they assign to Allah created anything like His creation so that their creation is similar to His? Say, 'Allah is the Creator of all things: He is the One, the All Compelling." *(13:16)*

"All this is Allah's creation. Now show Me what your other Gods have created." *(31:11)*

"Can He who creates be compared to one who cannot create?" *(16:17)*

"Those they invoke beside Allah create nothing; they are themselves created." *(16:20)*

"The disbelievers take beside Him gods that create nothing and are themselves created." *(25:3)*

There are many other Qur'anic verses with similar messages, and they are enough to prove the case.

The point is that when a person observes the Decree of Allah Almighty, The Wise, in terms of sins and crimes, he realises that there is no one who can save and remove the causes of His anger except Him. There is no way to obey Him except with His help and no source to achieve His pleasure except His support. All things originate from Him and return to Him. The causes of support are in His hands and there is no other being except Him to whom the servants can take resort, or put their trust in him. The speaker of the prophets, Shu'ayb ﷺ declared as mentioned in Qur'an:

"I cannot succeed without Allah's help: I trust in Him, and always turn to Him." *(11:88)*

7. THE DIVINE NAMES AND ATTRIBUTES OF ALLAH

These are the most splendid, and higher than all the previous features. To realise it, leads to the understanding of the relation of the existence with the Beautiful Names and Lofty Attributes in creation and command. It is the most sublime and honourable knowledge. Every name of the Lord has a particular character. His names are the description of praise and perfection, and every attribute has a requirement and an act which is attached to one of its results. All this is connected with His creation and command, reward and punishment, and they are the result of His beautiful names.

It is impossible to detach His names from their descriptions and meanings, and detach the works from their effects. It is also unthinkable to detach the effects from His works and His works from His Attributes, and Attributes from His Names and His Names and Attributes from His essence.

Since His qualities are perfect and His works are based on wisdom and interest and His Names are beautiful, it is impossible to detach them from their results. For this reason the Almighty, glory be to Him, condemns those who put Him out of action from His command and prohibition, and reward and punishment. It is something which is not proper for Him and He must be declared free from it. Anyone who says it, does not give Him His proper place and the honour which is due to Him. Allah said about the people who denied the prophethood and sending of the messengers and revelation of the books:
"They did not assess Allah as He should be when they said that Allah did not send down any book." *(6:91)*

Allah warned those who denied the resurrection and reward and punishment:
"These people have not appraised Allah with true appraisal while the earth entirely will be in His grip on the Day of Resurrection and the heavens are folded in His hand." *(39:67)*

He spoke about those who requested the equal treatment of righteous and wicked people and the believers and disbelievers:
"Do those who commit evil deeds really think that We will deal with them in the same way as those who believe and do righteous deeds, that they will be alike in their living and dying? How badly they judge." *(45:21)*

So, He declared that it was a bad thought unsuitable to Him, which His Names and Attributes do not accept. The Almighty also said:
"Did you think We had created you in vain, and you would not be brought back to Us? Exalted be Allah, the true King, there is no god but Him, the Lord of the Glorious Throne." *(23:115-116)*

He is above this type of guessing and imagination as it is incompatible with His Names and Attributes. There are many verses in the Qur'an which dismiss any idea that goes against the implication of His Names and Attributes, as it leads to impair His perfectness and power to act as a sovereign.

His names Al-Hamid (The Praiseworthy) and Al-Majid (The Honourable) for example, mean that He has not neglected human beings, and left them in vain with no function to receive commands or prohibition and free from reward and punishment. His name Al-Hakim (The Wise) also rejects it. His names Al-Hayy (The Ever Living) and Al-Malik (The King) do not imply that He is unable to act. The essence of life is to act and every living person is active. His Names Al-Khaliq (The Creator) and Al-Qayyum (The Ever Watchful) implies His being alive and active. His Attributes Al-Sami' (All Hearing)' and Al-Basir (All Seeing)' require something to be seen and heard, Al-Khaliq requires something which is created, and Al-Malik requires Him to act in His kingdom, administering it, giving and withholding, doing favour and justice deciding to give reward or punishment. His other names like Al-Barr, Al-Muhasin, Al-Mu'ti, Al-Mannan (having the meanings of being kind and benevolent) require objects to receive His generous favours.

When this much becomes clear then it is to be noted that among His Names are Al-Ghaffar (The Most Forgiving), Al-Tawwab (The One who accepts repentance) and Al-'Afuww (The Most pardoning) and all these require a sin to be forgiven, repentance to be accepted and crimes to be pardoned. Similarly Al-Hakim needs subjects where His wisdom can be seen.

The Lord, Exalted, loves His essence, His names and Attributes. He is Most Forgiving, loves forgiving and pardoning and loves repentance. He is pleased with the servants when they return to Him in repentance with humility and sincerity. The magnitude of what He forgives and pardons, and relieves the offender of his crimes, is an essential requirement of His Names and Attributes. Acquisition of what He agrees with is the sign of His perfection. He praises Himself and so do the residents of the heavens and the earth as an acknowledgement of the perfection of His favours.

He is Al-Hamid and Al-Majid (The Most Praiseworthy and The Most Glorious), which require their effects. Among their effects are the forgoing of mistakes, abolition of slips, pardoning of the sins and tolerance of offences while He has full power to exact the dues and knows the offence and its punishment. His toleration after knowing, forgiving after having power and condoning the shortcomings, all are the outcome of His perfect might and wisdom. The Messiah, son of Maryam peace be on him, said:

"If You punish them, they are Your servants; if You forgive them, You are the Mighty, the Wise". *(5:118)*

The meaning is that Your forgiveness is the result of Your complete power and wisdom. It is not like the one who forgives because of incapacity, and condones out of ignorance of the dues. You are well aware of Your due, have power to exact them and are Wise in punishment.

If a person pays attention to diffusion of the Divine Names and Attributes in the world and in the commands, he will realise that the cause of the overlooking of these offences is from the servant. It is the requirement of His Lordship and Divinity.

In all His decrees there is a clear wisdom, and open signs. Through these decrees he wants to make the servants understand His Names and Attributes. He encourages them to love Him, remember and thank Him and devote themselves to Him through His beautiful Names. Every Name has special act of devotion, by knowing and understanding it and acquiring the essence of it. The perfect person in devotion is the one who approaches Allah with all the Names and Attributes that are known to human beings. Any particular devotion does not bar him from devotion through another one. The devotion by the Most Powerful, for example should not deter a person from approaching Him through the Clement and Merciful, or the Grantor from the Withholder, or the Merciful, the Forgiving and Pardoning from the Capable of exacting the penalty, or the Names denoting the concept of love, kindness, benevolence and favour from the Names of justice, power, greatness and might.

This is the way of the ideal marcher to Allah, and it is derived from the Qur'an. Allah, the Exalted, said:

"The Most Excellent Names belong To Allah: use them to call upon Him." *(7:180)*

Calling upon Him includes to supplicate, to praise and to show devotion. He, the Most High, invites His servants to know Him with His Names and Attributes, praise Him with them and take their shares from their devotion.

Allah, the Glorious, loves the requisite of His Names and Attributes. He is the All Knowing and loves people of knowledge. He is Generous and loves every generous man. He is Unique and loves uniqueness. He is Beautiful and loves beauty, is Forgiving and loves forgiveness and forgiving people, is Modest and loves modesty, is Kind and appreciates kindness, is Appreciative and likes thanks, is Patient and loves patience, is Clement and likes clemency. Because of His love of repentance and forgiveness He created those whom He may forgive, who turn to Him so that He may pardon them. He decreed causes of matters happening, He dislikes and disproves so that He can show concern what He likes and approves.

The causes in relation to their effects are of four types: A desired one that leads to the desired effect, a hateful one that leads to a hateful effect. These two are the cardinal factor for His decrees in relation to what He loves or dislikes. Then the third is a hateful cause, that leads to hateful effects and a desired one that leads to undesired results. These last two are impossible with respect to Him. The desired objectives are by His decrees and decision. He created what He created and decreed what He decreed for the servants in order to reach them. They, therefore, must be desired and appreciable to the Lord, the Excellent. Some causes leading to those objectives are desired and some hateful to Him.

Obedience and Tawhid are loved causes for Him. They lead to kindness and reward which are loved by Him. Shirk and sins are hateful causes which lead to justice which He likes though He loves favour more than justice. A combination of favour and justice is more preferable to Him than one of them alone because they together include perfect sovereignty, praise and complete power.

This position is too great to be included in full in a book or to be comprehended in one discourse. We have just made a gesture to reveal what is behind it. Allah is the supporter and helper.

8. SUPPORT AND DESERTION

This is the completion of the previous position, but has been singled out for the need of the servant to understand it and benefit from it. Those who are aware of Allah's attributes know that 'Tawfiq,' the support of Allah, means that He does not surrender you to yourself, opposite of it is desertion of Him and leaving you to yourself. All the servants stroll between His support and desertion. Even in one period a man gets his share of both, when the Almighty gives to him and makes him happy, and in return he remembers Him and thanks Him for His support. The he disobeys and violates His commands and makes Him angry because He leaves him alone. In this way a man moves between His help and desertion. If He helps him, it is from His mercy and grace, if He deserts him, it is because of His justice and wisdom. In both cases He is praised fully and completely. He did not deprive the servant of something which belonged to him. He in fact barred him from it because of His grace and benevolence. He knows well where to put His benevolence.

When the servant understands this position properly, he will realise the importance of it and his need in every moment for the help and support of Allah, the Great. He will also know that his belief and Tawhid are in the hands of Allah Almighty. If he moves from it for a second, the throne of his Tawhid will crumble and the sky of his faith will fall to the ground. The one who holds it is the same One who restrains the sky from falling on the earth. His heart and tongue are busy in repeating, "O Turner of the hearts, keep my heart firm on Your religion. O Regulator of the hearts, set my heart on Your obedience." He cries, "O Ever-Living, Ever-watchful, Originator of the heavens and the earth, the Owner of honour and power, there is no God but You. I seek refuge in Your mercy. Put right all my affairs and do not entrust me to myself or to any of Your creation for a twinkling of an eye."

The servant in this state witnesses the support and desertion of Allah as he witnesses His Lordship and His creation. He asks Him like a person in need and takes refuge in Him like a desperate person. He throws himself before Allah Almighty, surrendering himself, putting his head in front of Him, in the position of humbleness, servility and submissiveness. He knows that he does not have power to cause harm or benefit for him, nor is he able to cause death or life or resurrection.

Tawfiq (support) of Allah means His will to guide His servant what can put his affairs right and to make him able to do what will make Him pleased, turning him to Himself, putting His love above anything else. He makes him hate and abhor what displeases Him. This is the act of Allah which He does to His servant. He said:

"But Allah has endeared to you the faith and has made it pleasing in your hearts and has made hateful to you disbelief, defiance and disobedience. They are those who are rightly guided. It is a bounty from Allah and a favour. Allah is All-Knowing, All-Wise." *(49:7-8)*

It is He, glory belongs to Him, who knows who deserves this favour and who does not. He is wise and endows favour to its deserving people. He does not keep it from those who deserve it and does not confer on those who are not qualified. He said it after saying:

"Be aware that Allah's Messenger is among you; if he obeys you in many cases you certainly suffer." *(49:7)*

Then He rectified it by saying: "But Allah endeared faith to you."

The Almighty wants to say that your love of faith and its intention and making it beautiful in your hearts was not from you. It was Allah who did it and you found it pleasing. Therefore do not put yourselves before His Messenger, do not speak until he does and do not do anything until he asks to do it. The One who has endeared faith in your hearts knows better than you what is good for His servants. If Allah's help was not with you, you would not have been able to believe. Your belief was not by your decision and you did not approach it by your own will. Your souls were unable to reach it. Now if His Messenger obeyed you in many matters as you wished, you would have suffered seriously and your good deeds would have been lost without you perceiving it. Do not have conjecture that your souls wish excellence and success for you. If it were not that He endeared it to you and made it beautiful to your hearts and made its opposite hateful to you, it would not have happened. And your souls would have not accepted it.

Here is an example to illustrate support and desertion. A king sent a messenger to a town with a message that the enemy is going to attack it very soon. He will destroy the town and the people. The king also dispatched money, vessels, equipments, supplies and experts. He advised them to march, saying that he had sent all that they needed. He also ordered some of his slaves to go to so-and-so and pick him up and not to let him stay there. He gave similar orders concerning other people, but to leave others because they did not deserve to stay in his kingdom. The special envoys left and picked and carried those who they were ordered to carry and brought them to the king. After that the enemy attacked those who remained in the town and killed and arrested them.

Will this king be considered to be unjust to those people? It is true that he chose some people for his protection and care, yet deserted others. He is not obliged to treat them with equity by his favour. It was his bounty to give to whomever he wished.

The *Qadariyyah* and *Jabariyyah* explained the support by creation of obedience, and desertion by creation of disobedience. They built it on their false principles of denying the causes and wisdom, and referred the matter to the will of Allah without any cause or wisdom. The *Qadariyyah* who deny the attributes of Allah explained their support by general statements and guidance. They said that it was the ability to obey and provide its sources, which is available to every disbeliever and polytheist who received the message and had ability to believe.

The Divine support in their view is a common thing between the disbelievers and the believers. Guidance, manifestation, and giving power are shared by both groups. It was not only believers who were given this support which made them believe. In the same way the disbelievers were not deserted and stopped from believing. If it was so, it would have been injustice and partiality. They kept up to this principle and derived false basis' for their views.

Allah, the Mighty and Wise, guided those who believed in the truth, concerning that which others had differed. Allah guides the one whom He wishes to the right path. They did not follow the way of this and that because they knew that both have deviated from the right course. They affirmed Divine Decree and destination and believed that Allah's will encompasses all the universe. They also asserted the cause and wisdom, the goal and interest. They put Allah, the Most High, above being unable to give power to His creation over things that do not fall under His power. They do not believe that any of the acts of mankind can take place without the will of Allah. If anyone says it, he has not known his Lord and has not fully recognised His Lordship.

They also declared the Almighty above doing what is bad and futile, or creating something without purpose. They also believe that all His acts are full of wisdom, for which He created them. He also set causes and effects: all these have great wisdom. This wisdom is an established eternal attribute of Him, and not created, as the *Qadariyyah* claim.

The people of the right path are free from both groups, except in matters which include the truth. They do not reject any truth which their statements contain. They are the witnesses and custodians of Allah on all groups. They are the judge over them and are not to be judged by them. Only such people are able to expose the truth, who have good knowledge of what the Messenger of Allah ﷺ has brought, and can recognise the difference between his teachings and false claims. They are the selected and elite among the people. They do not belong to those who divided their religion and became sects, and split their matters. They belong to those who have clear evidence from their Lord, have good understanding of their faith and have knowledge of what others have.

Allah is the helper.

9. INCREASE IN FAITH AND ITS EVIDENCE

This is the most delicate subject, which suits the people of knowledge. The reader may rush to reject it, asking how the faith can increase by sins and offences. They are the cause of decreasing faith. The early scholars have unanimously agreed that faith increases with good deeds and decreases with disobedience. Here you have to understand that this happens with the attention of the learned man to the sins committed by him or others and to their effects. The effects of these sins are a sign of the prophethood. It is amongst the evidences of the truthfulness of the Messengers and the authenticity of their messages.

The Messengers, may Allah's blessings and peace be upon them, commanded the servants to follow what is good for them in their outer and inner conditions, and what is useful to their lives and in the Hereafter. They prohibited what contained the damage of the inner and outer of their affairs and loss of their world and the Hereafter. They informed people about what Allah liked and appreciated and what He disliked and abhorred. They said that if He is obeyed in what He had commanded, He would appreciate and grant additional bounty and benefit in the hearts, bodies and wealth. The servant will notice this increase and strength in all his conditions. On the other hand if the Lord is disobeyed in His command and prohibitions, it will result in loss, weakness, disgrace, distress, anguish and misery. Allah, the Exalted, said in the Qur'an:

"Whoever, male or female, does good deeds and has faith, We shall give him a good life and reward them according to the best of their actions." *(16:97)*

"Say, (Allah says), believing servants, be mindful of your Lord! Those who do good deeds in this world will have a good reward." *(39:10)*

"Ask your Lord for forgiveness, then turn back to Him. He will grant you wholesome enjoyment until an appointed time, and give His grace to everyone who has merit." *(11:3)*

"Whoever turns away from My remembrance will have a life of great hardship, and We will bring him blind to the Assembly on the Day of Resurrection." *(20:124)*

Some people interpreted "hardship" with the torment of the grave. But the correct meaning is that it is in this world. Anyone who turns away from the reminder which Allah sent down will suffer from the annoyance, hardship of life, abundance of fear and intense greed of the world and discomfort in running after it. It also includes the distress which he suffers when he fails to get what he wanted or loses after acquiring it. He does not feel the pain he goes through in his attempt to acquire it because he is completely intoxicated. When he recovers for a while, he feels pain and tries to remove it by taking another dose. This is how he passes his life in agony. What a painful life is it if the heart is able to conceive it.

The hearts of the people involved in innovations and those who turn away from the Qur'an and those who are unmindful of Allah and are engaged in sinful deeds live in Hell before the great Hell. On the other hand the hearts of the righteous people enjoy the comfort before the great comfort.

"The righteous will live in bliss, and the wicked will burn in the Fire." *(82:13-14)*

This is in all three abodes and not only in the Hereafter, although the full torment will appear in the Hereafter. It will be less in the *Barzakh*, as Allah has said:
"For the evildoers there is a punishment before that (i. e. the Hereafter)." *(52:47)*

"And they say, "When is the fulfilment of this promise if what you say true? Say, 'Maybe some of what you seek to hasten is near at hand." *(27:71-72)*

In this world there is less trouble and pain than the *Barzakh*, but it is not felt because of the dominance of the desires which keeps the heart away from thinking about it. A servant may be afflicted with physical pain, but would like to ignore it and divert his attention from it. He would like to think about other things in order to escape from feeling it. If his attention is moved to the pain, he would yell for the severity of it. This is concerning the physical pain so what will be the case with the agony and suffering of the hearts?

Allah, the Glorious, has decreed for the good deeds and obedience a rewarding and pleasing result. Their pleasure is far higher than the pleasure of committing the sin. Similarly, for offences and sins, the Lord has fixed painful effects and distress that exceed the enjoyment of committing them. Ibn Abbas said, "The good deed produces light in the heart, brightness on the face, strength in the body, increase in the provision and love in the hearts of the people. On the other hand the sinful act results in blackness on the face, darkness in the heart, weakness in the body, decrease in the provision and hatred in the hearts of the people."

It is known to the people of insight; they realise them in themselves and others.

No one is faced with a painful condition without committing a sin, and what Allah forgives is much more. He, the Most High, said:
"Whatever misfortune befalls you, it is because of what your own hands have done - and Allah forgives much." *(42:30)*

The Almighty said to the best of His servants, the Companions of His Messenger:
"Why did you say, when a disaster struck you, even after you had inflicted twice as much damage (on your enemy): 'How did this happen?' Say, 'You brought it upon yourselves.'" *(3:165)*

He also said:

"Anything good that happens to you is from Allah, anything bad is from yourself." *(4:79)*

Good and bad here mean the bounties and disasters that the servant gets from Allah. That is why the Almighty said 'Happen to you' and did not say 'What you were inflicted with.'

The cause of any disaster, evil and misfortune in this world and the Hereafter is sins and violation of the commands of Allah, the Most High.

All the troubles in the world are the result of sins and disobedience. The effects of the good and bad deeds in the hearts, bodies and wealth are an obvious matter which every man of reason can see. The believer and unbeliever, righteous and rebellious, all know it.

The realisation of it in himself and others makes the faith of the believer in what the messengers have brought, and the matter of reward and punishment strong. This is the justice which can be witnessed in this world. Immediate reward and punishment are great evidence for those who have insight. Some people said, "When an evil deed happens from me and I do not repent, I expect its bad result upon me. When I am inflicted more or less of what I had assumed I declare: 'I testify that there is no god but Allah, and I testify that Muhammad is the Messenger of Allah.'"

It is the evidence of faith. It is so because when the truthful Messenger give the instruction to perform something and a person acts on it but faces a difficult situation, consequently his faith will increase. This is not an option available to everyone. The hearts of most of the people are covered with sins and they do not feel anything of this sort. It is only noticed by a heart which has light of faith and is shaken intensely by the storms of desires for sins and crimes. It witnesses the combat of the lamp of his faith with those desires. This man feels like a traveller in the sea at the time of a raging storm. The storm turns the boat upside down, especially when it is broken and he is left on a board at the mercy of the winds. This is how a believer views himself at the time of committing a sin, if good is willed for him. Otherwise his heart will be in another valley.

When this door is open for the servant he benefits from observing the history of the world and the conditions of the nations and what happened to them. He even learns from watching what the people of his time go through. In this situation he understands the meaning of Allah's statement:

"Is he who stands over every soul marking its action?" *(13:33)*

"Allah bears witness that there is no god but Him, as do the angels and those who have knowledge, upholding justice. There is no god but Him, the Almighty, the All Wise." *(3:18)*

The things you witness in the universe in terms of evil, pain, punishment, drought and loss of life for you and others, are the manifestation of the justice of the Lord. It is the justice and fairness of Allah, even if it comes at the hands of an oppressor. The one who gave power to this oppressor is the Most Just.

Allah said concerning the corrupt people:
"We sent against you servants of Ours with great force, and they ravaged your homes."
(17:5)

Sins are like poison, harmful to the person. If he treats them with matching drugs, they will be subdued, otherwise they will overwhelm the power of the faith and the result will be destruction. Some earlier scholars said, "Sins are the courier of disbelief as the fever is the courier of death.'"

When the servant watches that after disobeying his Lord his condition has changed, the hearts are turned away from him, the doors are closed in his face, it is difficult to find a way and the members of his family - his children, wife and brothers - all look down upon him, he starts looking for the cause of this behaviour. When he discovers the cause, his faith becomes stronger. If he desists and applies the causes that oppose the previous condition, he will see respect after disgrace, happiness after grief, safety after fear and strength of the heart after it had lost its power. He can see the difference of the faith in his heart in the situations of obedience and disobedience. He is amongst the people about whom Allah has said:
"Allah will absolve them even of their worst deeds and will reward them according to their best." *(39:35)*

When the man in this situation looks at it and gives it his full consideration, he becomes one of the doctors of the hearts who knows their diseases and their treatment. He draws benefit from it and transfers it to whoever he wants amongst the creature of Allah. Allah knows best.

10. THE SITUATION OF MERCY

When a servant falls into a sin, the rigidity and hardness and state of anger which he has for the person who did wrong to him, departs from his heart. He was so enraged that if he had power, he would have killed him. He even prayed to Allah to destroy him for the sake of Allah and with the desire of eradicating the disobedience of Allah. He does not have mercy in his heart for sinners and offenders. He looks down with disdain at them and disparages, condemns and defames. If Allah's Decree comes in force and he is left alone with his souls, he seeks help from Allah and takes refuge in Him. He lies in unrest before Him like a man bitten by a snake, and calls upon Him like a man in need. That hardship for the sinners changes into delicacy and the roughness into mercy and softness. His curse against them turns into prayer for them and he asks Allah to show mercy on them and forgive them. What a useful situation and how great its benefit! Allah knows best.

11. THE CONDITION OF WEAKNESS AND INCAPACITY

This is the result of the previous condition. It leads a person to believe that he is incapable of protecting himself. He is very weak and has no power, no strength except with his Lord. He finds his heart like a feather thrown in a desert, turned right and left by the winds. Or like a traveller on a boat in the sea, with furious storms and strong waves which raise the boat up and bring it down. He feels that the rules of the Decree are in work for him. He is like a tool put flat before his master, thrown at his door, putting his face on the ground at his gate. He has no power to cause harm or bring benefit for himself nor can he cause death or bring life or produce resurrection. He feels that he has no more than ignorance and wrongdoing and their consequences. Destruction is closer to him than the string of his shoes, and he is like a goat cast before wolves and beasts and can be saved only by the shepherd. If the shepherd abandons him for even just a second, the beasts will tear him to pieces.

This is like the situation of the servant who is thrown between Allah and his enemies, the devils of humans and Jinn. If protected by Allah, they will not get access to him, but if He leaves him alone and entrusts him to himself for a moment, he will not be saved and become the share of the one who gets hold of him.

In this position the servant knows himself and eventually recognises his Lord. This is one of the explanations of the famous saying, "Whoever knew their own self, knew his Lord."

This is not a Hadith of the Messenger of Allah ﷺ but a statement from *Israiliyat* (writings of people of the book) in the following form: "O man, know yourself, you will know your Lord."

It has been given the following three interpretations:

1. Whoever knows his weakness will recognise the power of Allah. Whoever knows his own inabilities will recognise the strength of his Lord. If a man knows his humbleness, he will realise the majesty of his Lord, and if someone realises his ignorance, will know the knowledge of his Lord. Allah, the Most Glorious, has taken exclusive possession of the whole perfectness, praise, greatness and self-sufficiency while the servant is imperfect, poor and needy. The more the servant is aware of his imperfectness, faults, needs, humbleness and weaknesses the more he will be aware of his Lord's qualities of perfectness.

2. When a person looks at the good qualities such as power, will, speech and life, he will come to understand that the One who granted these qualities to him deserves them more. The giver

of the perfectness is more entitled to perfectness. How can a person enjoy having life, the power of speech, hearing, seeing, knowing and doing what he wishes by his will, yet the One who created him and gave all this to him will not have these powers? It is totally unthinkable. In fact the One who made His servant able to speak deserves to be the speaker in the first place. The One who gave him life, knowing, hearing, seeing and doing things by his will is more entitled to possess these qualities. The first interpretation belongs to the section of contrast and the second one to that of preference.

3. This is part of the negation. It means that you are unable to know yourself which is nearer to you, but if you do not understand its essence and the nature of its qualities, how can you understand your Lord and the nature of His qualities?

The point is that this position makes the servant aware of his failure and weakness. This will result in the removal of the frivolity of claims and attributing matters to himself. He will realise that he has no power over anything, and he is incapable, weak and impotent.

12. THE POSITION OF HUMBLENESS AND SUBMISSION

The previous situation will lead to this position, which is made up of disgrace, lowliness, submission and the need of the Lord, the Sublime. He will notice in every part of his secret and open matters complete dependence on his Lord, and Guardian and the One who holds the matters of his success, guidance and happiness. This feeling which appears in his heart cannot be expressed in words. It can only be realised. His heart will acquire an unmatched submission. He will see himself as a pot which is broken on the ground. There is nothing in him, by him or from him. He owns no benefit and is not a subject of interest for others. He is in need of a new setting by his Creator and Caretaker. In this situation he will receive more benefit from his Lord while knowing very well that he did not deserve anything from Him. Any benefit he receives from Allah he will consider it too much for him. He will feel that his rank is below what he gets. It was the mercy of his Lord which brought it to him. His good deeds, even if they are equal to the obedience of the man and Jinn are the least that he has to do for his Lord. The little offences and shortcomings will be perceived as significant by him. All this is produced by the lowliness which dominated his heart.

How close is the setting for this broken heart! How close are the help, mercy and provision from him! How useful is this situation for him! A tiny bit of it is dearer to Allah than the huge good deeds like mountains from those who are proud and conceited by their deeds, their knowledge and their conditions. The most beloved heart to Allah, the Exalted, is that in which this humility has taken place, and submission has dominated it. His head is bowed before his Lord; he does not raise it because of shame and embarrassment from Allah.

One of the perfect persons in knowledge was asked, "Does the heart bow down in prostration?" He replied, "Yes, it falls in prostration and does not raise his head to the Day of meeting with Allah."

This is the prostration of the heart. A heart which lacks this humility does not bow down in that desired prostration. When the heart falls down in this great prostration, all parts of the body will follow. All the faces will be humbled before the Living and Ever Watchful One, and the voices and limbs will be hushed. The servant will show humility, submissiveness and lowliness. He will put his cheek on the doorstep of the servitude, looking by his heart at his Lord and Guardian, like a humble person looking at the Mighty and the Merciful One. He will be seen flattering, begging for the mercy and sympathy of his Lord. He will be engaged in trying to please his Lord as a perfect lover entreats his beloved owner without whom he cannot survive. He has no way but to please him and earn his sympathy because his life and success depend on his pleasure and love. He asks, "how can I make angry the one with whose pleasure is my life? How can I turn away from the one in whose love and remembrance are my happiness and success?"

The person in this position sees himself like a man who was in the care of his father. He provided him with the best food, drink and clothing, and educated him in the best way. He tried to make him reach the highest degree of perfection, and took care of all his interests. Then his father sent him on an errand. On his way he was attacked by an enemy who captured him and tied him firmly, then took him to the country of the enemies and subjected him to terrible torment, opposite to the treatment of his father. He remembered from time to time the care and favour of his father and felt ardent regret in his heart for missing his father's love and care. When in the custody of his enemy, who subjected him to all sorts of torment and decided in the end to kill him, his attention was turned to the country of his father and he saw him nearby. He rushed to him and threw himself before him and lay flat on the ground crying, "Father, father, father! Look what happened to your son!" The father hugged him and took him in his arms. His enemy was searching for him, and eventually found him in his father's arms. Do you think that the father will surrender the son to his enemy? Surely not! Then what do you think about the One who is more affectionate to His servant than a father to his son and a mother to her child?

Whenever a servant flees to Allah ﷻ and runs away from his enemy, throws himself at His door, rubbing his face in the dust of His gate, crying, "My Lord! My Lord! Show mercy to a man who has no other person to pity him, no helper beside You, no shelter beside You and no refuge but in You. I am Your destitute and poor servant, begging and putting my hopes in You. There is no refuge or security from You except in You. You are this servant's shelter and protector. O the One to whom I turn in what I hope, and take refuge in Him from what I fear; no one can settle the bone You broke and no one can break it when You set it," he then proceeds to the next stage.

13. THE SCENE OF DEVOTION, LOVE AND DESIRE TO MEET ALLAH

When the devotee reaches the previous stage and his heart is fixed with it and he tastes the flavour and sweetness of it, he proceeds to the stage of devotion, love, desire to meet Allah and feeling happy and pleased with Him. The servant's eyes are cooled by Him, his heart finds peace in Him, and his limbs feel assured in His protection. His remembrance flows on his tongue and heart. The thoughts of love take place of the thoughts of disobedience. The desire of coming closer to Him and achieving His pleasure replace the desire of disobeying and displeasing Him. His tongue and limbs move toward the good deeds instead of bad ones. His heart is filled with His love, his tongue utters His praise and his limbs move to His obedience. This humility has a unique impact in love which cannot be expressed in words.

One of the devoted men said, "I approached Allah from every door of good deeds but found it crowded and could not manage to enter, until I came from the door of humility and need. I found it the closest door and the widest one to reach Him. There is no crowd and no barrier. As soon as I put my foot at the doorstep, He, glory be to Him, held my hand and admitted me to His presence."

Shaykh al-Islam Ibn Taymiyyah, may Allah be pleased with him, used to say, "If a person wishes to have eternal happiness, he should stick at the doorstep of the devotion."

A very devoted person once said, "There is no way closer to Allah than through His adoration and there is no thicker barrier than false claims. Deeds and hard work are of no use if there is arrogance and conceit. Inactivity is not harmful with humility and submission." He meant after performing the obligatory duties.

The point is that this humility and submissiveness bring the servant to Allah and set him on the path of love. A special door is opened for him, which is not opened by any other means, although all good deeds and acts of obedience open doors of love for the servant. But the door opened through humility, submissiveness, contempt against his own soul and seeing it as weak and incapable, blaming and discrediting it, and looking at its mistakes and shortcomings is another type of opening. The person who takes this path is unusual amongst the people. There is a deep gulf between him and others. This route is known as the route of flying, in which the man sleeping on his bed goes ahead of those who run. He makes great progress and goes ahead of the others. Even while he is talking to you, he goes out of sight and surpasses those trying to compete in the field of devotion.

Allah's help is sought and He is the best of Forgivers.

A devout servant succeeded in achieving all these good results of the love of Allah, which was due to his repentance, which made Allah happy. He, the Most High, loves those who turn to Him in repentance and is pleased immensely by it. Whenever the servant witnesses the kindness, clemency and favour of Allah to him before committing the sin and during and after it, his heart is stirred up with the love of the Almighty and a desire to meet Him. It is because the hearts are made to love those who do favour to them. Which favour is greater than the favour of the One who treats the servant involved in sin? Despite his disobedience He shows His grace to him, treats him kindly and provides him with many forms of protection. He gives him protection against his enemies, who wait for an opportunity to grab a small mistake and use it for disparaging him. He, the Most Glorious, frustrates them and prevents their schemes. The servant watches all this by his own eyes. He had reached a position in which the heavens were asking their Lord for permission to pelt stones on him, the earth was about to make him sink and the sea was seeking permission to drown him. It is related in the Musnad of Imam Ahmad that the Prophet ﷺ said, "No day passes but the sea is seeking its Lord permission to drown the son of Adam, and angels look for the permission to deal with him and destroy him, but the Lord Almighty says, 'Leave My servant to Me; I know him better. I produced him from the earth. If he is your servant, you have right to deal with him; but if he is My servant then his affairs are to Me. By My honour and greatness if My servant approaches Me at night, I will receive him. If he comes to Me in daytime, I will welcome him. If he comes near Me by a span of a hand, I will go to him by the length of an arm. If he comes to Me walking, I will go to him running. If he seeks forgiveness, I will forgive him, if he seeks abolition of his offences, I will do it for him and if he turns to Me in repentance, I will respond to him. Who is greater than Me in benevolence and kindness when I am the most Generous and Kind? My servants pass their nights committing major sins, still I protect them in their beds. Whoever proceeds to Me I receive him from far away. Anyone who leaves something reprehensible I grant him more than he expected. Whoever acts with My power and strength I make the iron soft for him. He who seeks what I want I will fulfil his wish. Those who remember Me are the people of My company, those who give thanks are the ones to whom I give more, and those who obey Me are the people of My honour. Those who are involved in committing sins, I do not disappoint them from My mercy. If they repent, I am their friend and if they do not, I am their physician. I afflict them with misfortunes in order to purify them from failings.'" *(Musnad Ahmad)*

Let us close the chapter of repentance, its rulings and its impacts. I did not deal at length with this matter but there is an excessive need for people to know about it, understand its requirements and the details of its rules. Allah is the helper in this regard and He is the One who can allow practicing them as He helped in understanding and knowing them. Whoever puts his trust in Him and takes refuge in Him will never be disappointed. There is no power, no strength except in Allah.

One has to remember that repentance includes all the stages of Islam. Every other matter is contained within it.

INDEX

'Asr: 50, 119, 120, 121, 123, 126
A'ishah: 25, 51, 125
Aaron: 109
Abu Hanifah: 57, 112, 114, 126, 131
Abu Jahl: 26, 81
Adam: 23, 61, 64, 65, 78, 110, 144, 145
Adultery: 25, 48, 51, 56, 57, 66, 75, 78, 79, 81, 86, 111, 112, 113, 115, 131, 133
Ahmad: 44, 51, 52, 57, 112, 114, 121, 126, 131, 134, 163
Al-'Afuww: 150
Al-'udwan: 114, 115
Al-baghy: 114, 115
Al-Barr: 32, 150
Al-Basir: 150
Al-Fahishah: 115
Al-Ghaffar: 33, 150
Al-Hakim: 149, 150
Al-Hamid: 149, 150
Al-ithm: 114, 115
Al-Khaliq: 150
Al-Mannan: 150
Al-Mu'ti: 150
Al-Muhasin: 150
Al-Sami': 150
Al-Shafi'i: 57, 112, 114, 125, 130, 131
Al-Tawwab: 150
Al-zulm: 115
Anas: 25, 34, 77, 78
Angels: 22, 23, 35, 44, 96, 105, 138, 143, 145, 157, 183
Annihilation: 12, 28, 61
Antidote: 61
Arafat: 120
Association: 46, 53, 66, 75, 76, 77, 79, 83, 87, 90, 96, 116, 132, 146

Barzakh: 20, 156
Beast: 59, 106, 139, 140, 159
Behaviour: 13, 18, 22, 28, 69, 79, 82, 92, 97, 98, 115, 141, 158
Benevolence: 24, 34, 37, 45, 85, 151, 152, 163
Blame: 18, 20, 21, 22, 32, 55, 113, 120, 122, 135, 137, 142

Bukhari: 78, 108

Caliph: 98
Canine: 138
Charity: 16, 38, 43, 50, 53, 106, 108, 127, 128, 129, 130, 131, 132
Clement: 32, 34, 144, 151
Companions: 10, 11, 27, 41, 55, 65, 75, 76, 79, 88, 92, 106, 107, 119, 121, 125, 126, 128, 131, 133, 141, 156
Conditions: 13, 18, 22, 30, 36, 64, 68, 120, 121, 122, 123, 138, 145, 155, 157, 160
Creator: 38, 39, 40, 44, 81, 83, 90, 96, 103, 141, 142, 146, 148, 150, 160

Dawud: 29, 59
Day of Judgement: 20, 63, 73, 77, 83, 127, 128, 137
Decree: 14, 15, 20, 21, 22, 25, 26, 27, 28, 31, 32, 33, 43, 44, 45, 62, 67, 95, 104, 136, 138, 141, 142, 143, 144, 146, 148, 150, 151, 154, 156, 158, 159
Devil: 15, 23, 35, 41, 42, 44, 78, 89, 110, 141, 145, 159
Disbelief: 12, 30, 39, 41, 47, 49, 50, 52, 53, 74, 78, 80, 87, 88, 89, 90, 102, 105, 108, 116, 127, 153, 158
Disbelievers: 20, 23, 48, 54, 84, 92, 97, 98, 100, 101, 103, 106, 107, 109, 134, 146, 148, 149, 154
Disobedient: 18, 47, 52, 60, 101, 108
Divine: 14, 20, 21, 65, 79, 80, 84, 98, 104, 123, 136, 141, 142, 144, 145, 146, 147, 148, 150, 154
Donkey: 99, 139

Evil: 14, 24, 39, 40, 43, 44, 50, 51, 53, 54, 56, 57, 58, 62, 64, 65, 66, 67, 70, 71, 79, 82, 99, 102, 103, 115, 128, 131, 135, 136, 139, 140, 142, 149, 157
Evildoers: 10, 23, 27, 89, 156

Fabrications: 86
Fahishah, 115
Falsehood: 50, 70, 101, 107, 110, 121
Forgiveness: 13, 14, 24, 30, 33, 34, 36, 39, 40, 42, 45, 46, 52, 54, 55, 57, 62, 64, 65, 69, 70, 71, 72, 75, 76, 77, 78, 79, 80, 83, 96, 111, 132, 133, 135, 137, 150, 151, 155, 163
Fornication: 54, 86

Gabriel: 106, 107
Glorious: 10, 11, 27, 29, 31, 37, 38, 39, 42, 44, 52, 72, 110, 113, 139, 143, 146, 149, 150, 151, 156, 159, 163
Guidance: 11, 39, 41, 42, 73, 74, 97, 99, 102, 111, 146, 160

Hadith: 10, 15, 28, 34, 44, 46, 50, 55, 65, 67, 77, 79, 80, 81, 88, 133, 159

Hearts: 17, 34, 63, 73, 83, 84, 93, 97, 98, 100, 102, 103, 104, 106, 107, 114, 142, 145, 146, 153, 156, 157, 158, 163
Humility: 13, 14, 18, 29, 33, 63, 67, 81, 95, 107, 138, 145, 150, 160, 161, 162
Hypocrisy: 53, 87, 89, 90, 96, 105, 106, 107
Hypocrites20, 43, 69, 84, 97, 101, 102, 103, 105, 106, 107, 111

Iblis: 23, 110
Ibn Taymiyyah: 57, 59, 82, 129, 130, 131, 142, 162
Ibrahim: 96, 144
Ignorance: 11, 12, 14, 21, 22, 38, 39, 46, 54, 55, 81, 90, 95, 97, 108, 110, 139, 150, 159
Ihsan: 68
Ijtihad: 120, 126
Illegal: 51, 57, 130
Imam Ahmad: 44, 51, 52, 121, 126, 131, 134, 163
Iman: 68
Immorality: 87, 107, 115
Injustice: 21, 22, 23, 38, 39, 44, 50, 53, 77, 88, 116, 141, 154
Innovation: 41, 77, 78, 86, 94, 105, 110, 116, 117, 142, 156
Intention: 17, 25, 29, 30, 31, 49, 54, 55, 56, 57, 68, 70, 71, 74, 79, 85, 88, 94, 110, 111, 126, 153,
Intercession: 77, 91, 92, 93, 94, 133
Intercessors: 82, 92
Invoke: 75, 148
'Isha: 109, 123
Islam: 12, 13, 20, 26, 30, 47, 49, 52, 53, 69, 76, 80, 90, 94, 97, 108, 127, 132
Israiliyat: 159
Istighfar: 69

Jahmiyya: 110
Jinn: 23, 24, 36, 83, 110, 159, 160
Jonah: 82, 86
Jurists: 60, 113, 129, 139
Ka'bah: 65, 120
Khawarij: 52, 110

Laziness: 60
Literalists: 118

'Ma'siyyah', 110

Madinah: 55, 113, 132

Maghrib: 109, 123, 126
Malik (Imam): 57, 113, 114, 126, 131
Marwah: 120
Mercy: 10, 11, 14, 18, 19, 23, 24, 30, 31, 35, 36, 37, 39, 45, 65, 69, 73, 76, 77, 80, 85, 96, 105, 120, 132, 138, 145, 146, 147, 152, 157, 158, 159, 160, 161, 163
Messenger: 10, 11, 14, 15, 20, 22, 23, 24, 25, 26, 27, 34, 35, 37, 39, 40, 41, 42, 43, 44, 46, 49, 50, 51, 53, 55, 57, 61, 66, 67, 68, 72, 75, 76, 77, 78, 79, 80, 82, 83, 84, 87, 89, 90, 91, 92, 93, 94, 95, 96, 97, 102, 106, 107, 108, 109, 110, 112, 117, 118, 119, 121, 124, 125, 126, 129, 131, 133, 134, 135, 137, 141, 143, 144, 149, 153, 154, 155, 156, 157, 159
Michael: 106, 107
Mina: 120
Monkey: 140
Moses: 82, 109, 143
Mosques: 94
Mouse: 139
Mu'tazilah: 50, 52, 110, 134
Muhammad: 72, 74, 77, 82, 88, 95, 106, 112, 157
Muharram: 120
Muslim (Sahih): 7, 72
Muslims: 13, 28, 31, 44, 47, 49, 53, 56, 76, 96, 97, 99, 111, 129, 137, 139
Musnad: 44, 82, 95, 121, 163
Muzdalifah: 120, 126

Negligence: 17, 18, 22, 25, 62, 118, 121
Nuh: 26, 27

Obedience: 18, 29, 31, 33, 35, 37, 38, 47, 50, 54, 61, 83, 86, 92, 93, 110, 126, 143, 156, 158, 160, 162
Oppression: 87

Paradise: 17, 20, 22, 35, 49, 51, 53, 62, 63, 64, 71, 72, 74, 77, 86, 133, 136
Peacock: 140
Pharaoh: 26, 33, 82, 89, 143
Pilgrimage: 48, 95, 96, 105, 119, 120, 123, 124
Polytheist: 81, 83, 84, 90, 91, 92, 93, 94, 95, 96, 116, 131, 154
Prayers: 72, 75, 84, 103, 106, 109, 118, 120, 123, 125, 126, 127
Pretension: 18, 94
Prophet: 13, 14, 16, 25, 26, 27, 29, 34, 39, 42, 44, 45, 46, 50, 52, 53, 55, 57, 62, 63, 65, 67, 69, 73, 75, 78, 79, 82, 84, 85, 86, 89, 91, 93, 94, 96, 103, 105, 106, 109, 119, 120, 121, 122, 123, 124, 125, 126, 129, 133, 147, 148, 163
Prostration: 63, 94, 95, 161

Punishment: 12, 15, 41, 24, 29, 35, 36, 37, 40, 45, 47, 49, 50, 52, 56, 70, 71, 73, 76, 81, 85, 86, 97, 110, 112, 113, 132, 135, 136, 144, 148, 149, 150, 156, 157, 158

Qadariyyah: 43, 44, 142, 154
Qiblah: 120, 121
Qur'an: 14, 22, 43, 44, 45, 50, 51, 52, 69, 79, 80, 94, 97, 98, 100, 101, 106, 125, 131, 132, 139, 148, 149, 151, 155, 156

Ramadan: 52, 72, 75, 120, 123, 125
Rawafid: 110
Remembrance: 17, 29, 30, 32, 33, 84, 101, 155, 161, 162
Reptiles: 139
Resurrection: 20, 51, 55, 56, 66, 73, 101, 131, 142, 149, 152, 155, 159
Retribution: 136, 137, 140
Revelation: 89, 97, 98, 99, 100, 101, 192, 104, 110, 149
Rules: 46, 48, 69, 88, 98, 104, 118, 120, 132, 136, 159, 163

Safa: 120
Satan: 11, 14, 15, 22, 26, 40, 41, 42, 43, 55, 67, 78, 108, 141, 142
Scholars: 41, 44, 47, 49, 51, 57, 58, 63, 65, 71, 75, 78, 88, 98, 109, 112, 116, 118, 125, 126, 127, 129, 131, 132, 134, 135, 136, 155, 158
Servants: 10, 14, 24, 28, 36, 37, 44, 45, 53, 55, 62, 64, 65, 72, 74, 80, 81, 89, 97, 101, 102, 104, 105, 113, 126, 127, 132, 144, 145, 147, 148, 150, 151, 152, 153, 155, 156, 158, 163
Shari'ah: 21, 58, 86, 113, 115, 119, 120, 123, 124, 125, 128, 130, 134
Shawwal:120
Shirk: 41, 44, 46, 53, 79, 80, 81, 83, 90, 91, 92, 94, 95, 96, 116, 117, 132, 151

Sin: 11, 12, 13, 15, 17, 19, 24, 28, 29, 30, 31, 32, 40, 41, 42, 46, 47, 48, 49, 50, 51, 52, 53, 54, 55, 56, 58, 60, 61, 62, 63, 64, 65, 66, 67, 68, 70, 71, 75, 76, 77, 78, 79, 80, 81, 82, 83, 86, 111, 113, 115, 116, 119, 120, 128, 131, 133, 150, 163
Sincerity: 29, 30, 31, 64, 67, 71, 83, 86, 100, 117, 150
Sodomy: 115, 140
Soothsayer: 88
Spiritual: 18, 64, 68
Submission: 11, 14, 63, 81, 83, 93, 94, 95, 96, 160, 162
Submissive: 18, 19, 33, 63, 152, 161, 162
Sunnah: 41, 42, 43, 44, 50, 51, 53, 77, 94, 98, 99, 100, 101, 102, 104, 110, 115, 117, 110, 125, 139, 142
Supererogatory: 124
Supplication: 28, 40, 63, 72, 78

Swine: 115, 140

Tawfiq: 152
Tawhid: 41, 45, 79, 80, 81, 83, 85, 91, 92, 94, 95, 96, 134, 138, 143, 145, 146, 151, 152
Tayammum: 119, 124
Thamud: 89, 143
Throne: 12, 65, 77, 82, 147, 149, 152

Tirmidhi: 66
Traditions: 94, 104
Transgression: 11, 30, 87, 99, 113, 114, 130, 142, 143

Unbelievers: 88, 89, 91
Unlawful: 56, 57, 78, 110, 127, 130

Violation: 12, 25, 26, 61, 110, 112, 157

Weakness: 14, 17, 18, 25, 59, 61, 83, 138, 155, 156, 159, 160
Worshipper: 26, 35, 40, 42, 81, 83, 91, 93

Zakat: 48, 52, 105, 119, 123, 124
Zaqqum: 102
Zuhr: 119 123, 125